Connecting Cultures Through Language

SHARELINGO ®

Intermediate 2

Doc: Intermediate 2   **Ver.: 20200405**   **Copyright 2020, ShareLingo**

About ShareLingo's Mission

The ShareLingo Project is a social enterprise based in Denver Colorado that specifically focuses on helping English and Spanish speakers meet and practice with each other. We will work with other languages "some day". The larger goal is to break down tension and barriers – to promote the idea that we can all live and work side-by-side regardless of race, religion, gender, sexuality, country of origin, or any other factor.

For more information about The ShareLingo Project's mission and goals, please order a copy of *Beyond Words* by ShareLingo's founder James Archer. All profits will help organizations that support and encourage diversity and inclusion.

Beyond Words was ranked #1 on Amazon in the category of Sociology of Race Relations and can help schools, hospitals, institutions, businesses, churches and our community in general.

http://bit.ly/ArcherBooks

Scan this code

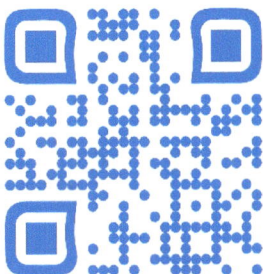

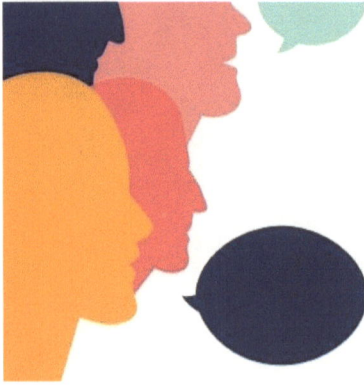

BIENVENIDO A SHARELINGO!

I don't take it lightly that you've invested in this program. And I can assure you that our team has been working nonstop to make this a world-class experience for you.

That's why I'm excited for you. This investment in ShareLingo marks the beginning of YOUR journey. So take comfort in that you are exactly where you need to be and you're surrounded by an absolutely incredible group of people who will support you to the end of that journey.

Now one thing you'll notice about ShareLingo is that we are very "hands on". Meaning, we are fully committed to your success and that means we are hyper engaged in all aspects of the course delivery. I tell you that because what you'll get from this experience is equal to what you put in.

Even more, you're now tapping into a community full of wisdom and insights as it relates to finally being able to speak Spanish with CONFIDENCE. That's why I encourage you to get to know the rest of the ShareLingo family. They are incredible and the communities they are working with are incredible too.

So welcome mi Amig@. It's going to be a blast and I'm so looking forward to supporting you through this amazing experience.

Saludos,

James Archer

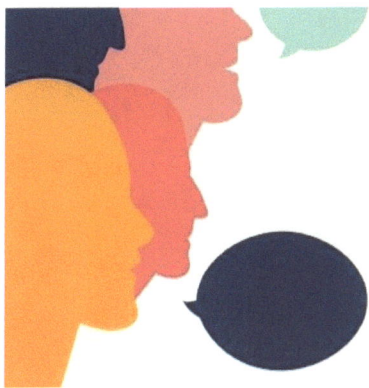

BIENVENIDO A SHARELINGO!

No tomo a la ligera que hayas invertido en este programa. Y puedo asegurarte que nuestro equipo ha estado trabajando sin parar para hacer de esto una experiencia de primera clase para usted.

Es por eso que estoy emocionado por ti. Esta inversión en ShareLingo marca el comienzo de TU viaje. Así que siéntete cómodo porque estás exactamente donde necesitas estar y estás rodeado por un grupo absolutamente increíble de personas que te apoyarán hasta el final de este viaje.

Ahora, una cosa que notarás sobre ShareLingo es que somos muy "prácticos". Es decir, estamos totalmente comprometidos con tu éxito y eso significa que estamos muy comprometidos con todos los aspectos de la entrega del curso. Te lo digo porque lo que obtienes de esta experiencia es igual a lo que pones.

Aún más, ahora estás aprovechando una comunidad llena de sabiduría y conocimientos en lo que respecta a finalmente poder hablar inglés con CONFIANZA. Es por eso que te animo a que conozcas al resto de la familia ShareLingo. Son increíbles y las comunidades con las que trabajan son increíbles también.

Así que bienvenido my friend. Va a ser una maravilla y estoy ansioso por apoyarte en esta increíble experiencia.

Saludos,

James Archer

The ShareLingo Project was developed to help people PRACTICE together.

For many people learning Spanish, the biggest barrier is not vocabulary or grammar… The biggest barrier is confidence speaking. And that means they just need more practice – with native speakers. Well, native Spanish speakers who want to speak English are in the same boat. They need confidence speaking too.

While the bilingual lessons in this book can certainly be used "stand alone", they were created as part of *The Spanish Success Path* course and membership developed by The ShareLingo Project.

ShareLingo developed and teaches a simple 4-part METHOD for English and Spanish speakers to use to practice together. This method ensures that both parties are getting "equal time" and that they can progress rapidly.

There are thousands of options for learning vocabulary and grammar – but what use are they if you still don't have any confidence speaking with native Spanish speakers?

If you would like more information about The ShareLingo Project, The Spanish Success Path, or the ShareLingo Method, please visit this link: www.iShareLingo.com

El proyecto ShareLingo fue desarrollado para ayudar a las personas a practicar juntos.

Para muchas personas que aprenden inglés, la barrera más grande no es el vocabulario o la gramática... La barrera más grande es hablar con confianza. Y eso significa que solo necesitan más práctica, con hablantes nativos. Bueno, los hablantes nativos de inglés que quieren hablar español están en el mismo barco. Necesitan confianza hablando también.

Si bien las lecciones bilingües en este libro pueden ser utilizadas "de manera independiente", se crearon como parte del curso y la membresía de El *Camino del Éxito de inglés* desarrollado por El Proyecto ShareLingo.

ShareLingo desarrolló y enseña un MÉTODO simple de 4 partes para que los hablantes de inglés y español lo usen para practicar juntos. Este método garantiza que ambas partes obtengan "el mismo tiempo" y que puedan progresar rápidamente.

Hay miles de opciones para aprender vocabulario y gramática, pero ¿de qué sirven si todavía no tienes confianza para hablar con hablantes nativos de inglés?

Si desea obtener más información sobre The ShareLingo Project, El *Camino del Éxito de inglés*, o El Proyecto ShareLingo, visite este enlace: www.iShareLingo.com/espanol

Course Description: ShareLingo was designed to help you improve your communication skills in your target language through different activities, such as personalized discussions, videos, readings, online exercises, etc.

We will help you:

- Understand your motivation for learning Spanish
- Find a Native Spanish speaker who you can practice with.
- Learn how to practice efficiently and effectively
- Enjoy the process

Things to remember:

- **We all have the ability to learn a new language.** If you can learn a new word in English, you can learn a new word in Spanish. It is the same part of the brain.

- To speak a new language, you need two things – foundation and practice.
- Foundation gives you the Vocabulary and Grammar. You can learn that "Good Morning" is "Buenos Dias".
- There are hundreds of places to build vocabulary and grammar. Classes, Online (like DuoLingo),

Descripción del curso: ShareLingo fue diseñado para ayudarle a mejorar sus competencias comunicativas en otro idioma, a través del desarrollo de diferentes actividades como discusiones personalizadas, videos, lecturas, ejercicios en línea, etc.

Le ayudaremos:

- Comprender su motivación para aprender español
- Encuentra un hablante nativo de inglés con quien puedes practicar
- Aprenda a practicar de manera eficiente y eficaz
- Disfruta del proceso

Cosas para recordar:

- **Todos tenemos la posibilidad y habilidad para aprender un nuevo idioma.** Si puedes aprender una nueva palabra en español, puedes aprender una nueva palabra en inglés. Es la misma parte del cerebro.

- Para hablar un nuevo idioma, necesita dos cosas: las bases fundamentales y la práctica.
- Las bases fundamentales te dan el vocabulario y la gramática. Puede aprender que "Buenos Días" es "Good Morning".
- Hay cientos de lugares para construir vocabulario y gramática. Clases, en línea (como DuoLingo),

CDs, Rosetta Stone, etc. Great. Do those. Begin!

- But if you want to speak with confidence to a real person – you have to PRACTICE with a real person. You won't have confidence saying "Buenos días" to someone until you have done it.

- Approaching someone to "test" your language skills can be scary, and is the one thing that holds the most people back. But unless you can practice, you are destined to fail. Remember high school?

- This is not just with language! Suppose you want to learn to play tennis. To really play, you have to practice with a PERSON.

- ShareLingo is the place to PRACTICE Spanish with a real person.

- Practice involves both LISTENING and SPEAKING.

- This program is different than any language program you have tried before.

- This program will teach you how to practice both listening and speaking with your partner.

CD's, Rosetta Stone, etc. Genial. Haz esos. ¡Comienza!

- Pero si quiere hablar con confianza a una persona real, tiene que PRACTICAR con una persona real. No tendrá confianza diciendo "Good Morning" a alguien hasta que lo haya hecho.

- Acercarse a alguien para "probar" sus habilidades de lenguaje puede ser aterrador, y es la única cosa que retiene a la mayoría de la gente. Pero a menos que pueda practicar, está destinado a fallar. ¿Recuerda la secundaria?

- ¡Esto no es sólo con el lenguaje! Supongamos que quiere aprender a jugar al tenis. Para jugar realmente, tiene que practicar con una PERSONA.

- ShareLingo es el lugar para PRACTICAR el inglés con una persona real.

- La práctica implica tanto ESCUCHAR y HABLAR.

- Este programa es diferente de cualquier programa de idioma que haya probado antes.

- Este programa le enseñará a practicar, tanto como a escuchar y a hablar con su compañero.

- It will also teach you how to FIND people to practice with you!

- ¡También le enseñará a ENCONTRAR personas a practicar con usted!

For your safety

Para su seguridad

THE SHARELINGO PROJECT encourages people from all walks of life to exchange their languages and cultures with other people.

While ShareLingo encourages daily interaction between participants, it is important for your safety that you only meet with other participants in a safe and public location.

Whenever you meet with a practice partner, remember that you do so at your own risk, and be careful.

El PROYECTO SHARELINGO anima a gente de todos los ámbitos de la vida a intercambiar su idioma y cultura con otras personas.

Si bien ShareLingo recomienda la interacción diaria entre los participantes, es importante para su seguridad que sólo se presente con otros participantes en una locación segura y pública.

Siempre que se reúna con un compañero de práctica, recuerde que lo hace bajo su propio riesgo, y tenga cuidado.

The ShareLingo Method
(working in pairs)

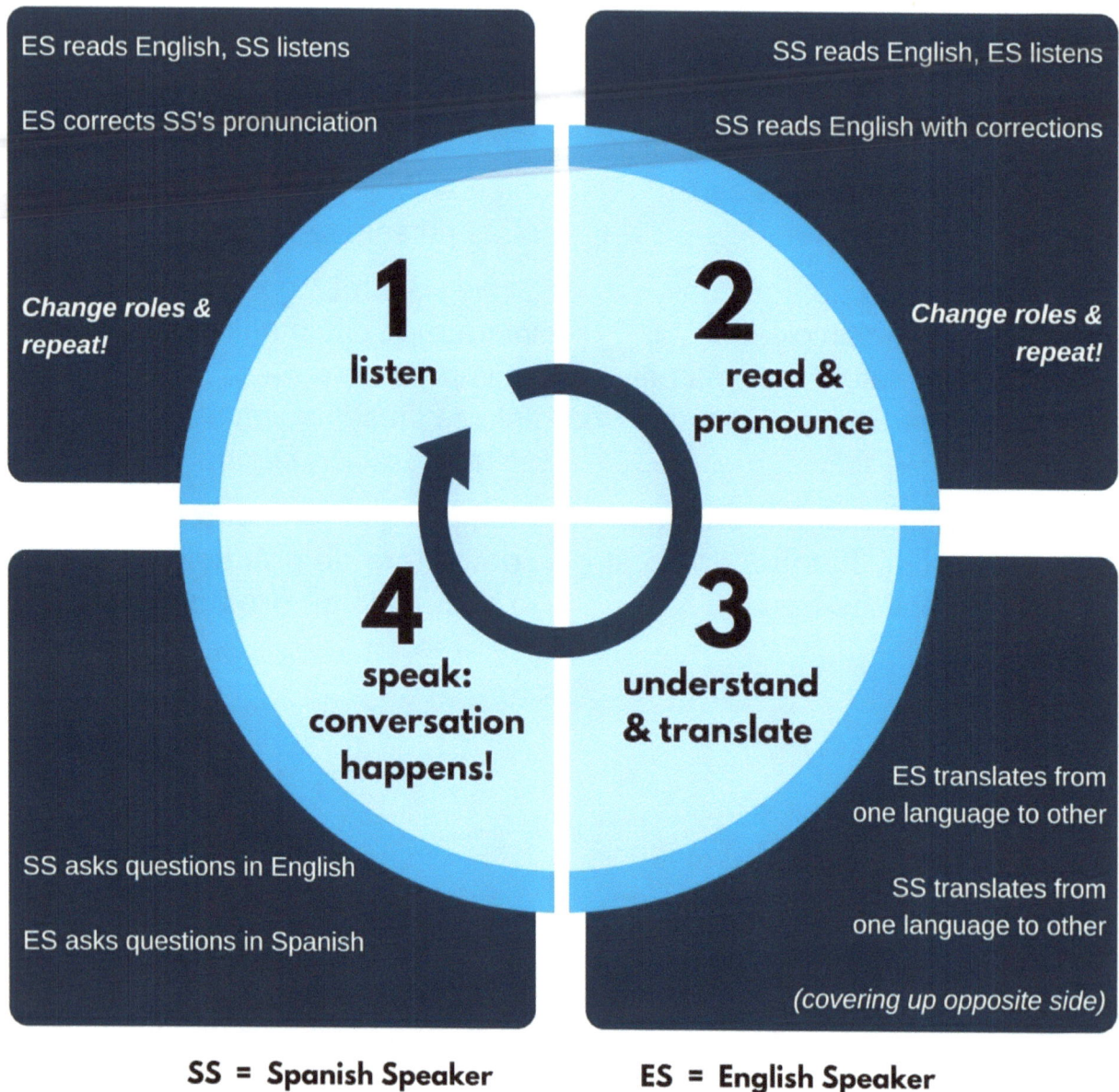

ES reads English, SS listens

ES corrects SS's pronunciation

Change roles & repeat!

1 listen

SS reads English, ES listens

SS reads English with corrections

2 read & pronounce

Change roles & repeat!

4 speak: conversation happens!

3 understand & translate

SS asks questions in English

ES asks questions in Spanish

ES translates from one language to other

SS translates from one language to other

(covering up opposite side)

SS = Spanish Speaker

ES = English Speaker

El Método de ShareLingo
(trabajando en parejas)

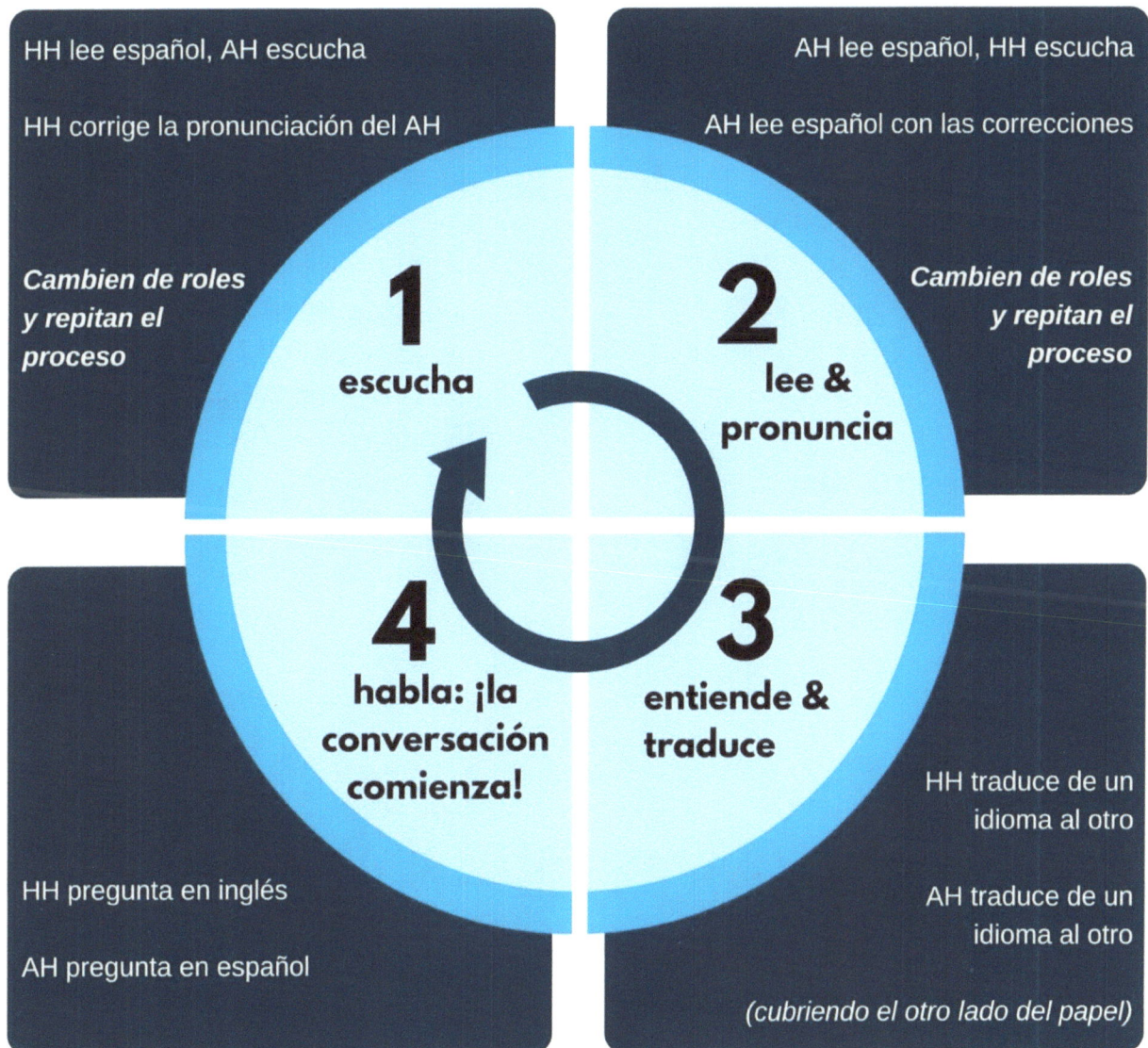

HH lee español, AH escucha

HH corrige la pronunciación del AH

Cambien de roles y repitan el proceso

AH lee español, HH escucha

AH lee español con las correcciones

Cambien de roles y repitan el proceso

1 escucha

2 lee & pronuncia

4 habla: ¡la conversación comienza!

3 entiende & traduce

HH pregunta en inglés

AH pregunta en español

HH traduce de un idioma al otro

AH traduce de un idioma al otro

(cubriendo el otro lado del papel)

HH = Hispanohablante   **AH = Anglohablante**

ShareLingo

LESSON OBJECTIVE

"If/then" statements, *"was going to ... but"*

OBJETIVO DE LA LECCIÓN

Frases de *"si… entonces"*, *"iba a … pero"*

VOCABULARY

1. I/he/she was going to
2. if I/he/she had
3. I/he/she would go
4. if I/he/she could
5. I/he/she would do
6. but
7. I/he/she would want
8. I would like to
9. if it were possible

VOCABULARIO

1. yo/él/ella iba a
2. si (yo/él/ella) tuviera
3. (yo/él/ella) iría
4. si (yo/él/ella) pudiera
5. (yo/él/ella) haría
6. pero
7. (yo/él/ella) querría / quisiera
8. (A mí/a él/a ella le) Me gustaría
9. si fuera posible

SHORT STORIES

1. I was going to go to my friend Michelle's house, but at that moment my mom called me on the phone and asked me if I could pick up some fresh eggs from grandmother. I thought to myself "If the eggs were fresh, I would do it, but the eggs aren't fresh." Also, if I had the money, I would go buy something else for her.
2. I told my mom that I would rather go shopping for something more exciting. She said that if she won the lottery she would send me shopping for something else but right now she would rather have the eggs.
3. If I could talk and say everything that I feel, I would talk, but I can only dance and express with my body what I feel. I was going to talk but I remembered that I would rather dance. At the end of the day I am better at dancing than I am at talking.
4. If I had enough guts, I would give a speech in front of a million people, but I only know how to talk to my friends.

5. If it were possible, we would travel to New York and then to another place. I would like to travel if I could.
6. I was going to pay the rent, but I decided to spend the money throwing a party instead. She would go to the concert with you if she didn't have to pay the rent for her friend who spent the money to pay for the party.

HISTORIAS CORTAS

1. Iba a ir a la casa de mi amiga Michelle, pero justo me llamó por teléfono mi madre y me preguntó "¿puedes llevarle unos huevos frescos a la abuela?". Pensé; si los huevos fueran frescos lo haría, pero los huevos no están frescos. Es más, si tuviera el dinero iría a comprar algo distinto para ella.
2. Le dije a mi mamá que preferiría ir de compras por algo más emocionante. Dijo que si se ganara la lotería me mandaría a comprar algo más, pero por ahora ella preferiría tener los huevos.
3. Si pudiera hablar y decir todo lo que siento, hablaría, pero sólo puedo bailar y expresar con mi cuerpo lo que siento. Iba a hablar, pero recordé que preferiría bailar. Al final de cuentas soy mejor bailando que hablando.
4. Si tuviera las agallas suficientes podría dar un discurso frente a un millón de personas, pero solo se hablar con mis amigos.
5. Si fuera posible, iríamos de viaje a Nueva York y después a otra parte. Si pudiera me gustaría viajar.
6. Iba a pagar la renta, pero decidí gastarme el dinero en una fiesta en su lugar. Ella iría al concierto contigo si no tuviera que pagar el arriendo para su amigo quien gastó su dinero para pagar la fiesta.

CLASS ACTIVITIES

What are some of your most common "buts?" Fill in the following blanks creating the situations.

1. I was going to _____,
   but _____.
2. He _____
   but _____.
3. She _____
   but _____.
4. We _____
   but _____.
5. They _____
   but _____.

We all have different "buts" that would stop us from doing what we want. What would stop you from enjoying a day out with friends?

The weather?
Lack of time/money?
Illness?
Disposition?

Share with your classmates a recent situation that you experienced where you wanted to do something, but something else interfered with your plans.

_____
_____

ACTIVIDADES PARA LA CLASE

¿Cuáles son tus "peros" más comunes? Llena los espacios para crear las situaciones respectivas.

1. Yo iba a _____,
   pero _____.
2. Él _____
   pero _____.
3. Ella _____
   pero _____.
4. Nosotros _____
   pero _____.
5. Ellos _____
   pero _____.

Todos tenemos distintos "peros" que nos impiden hacer lo que queremos. ¿Qué te impediría disfrutar un día afuera con tus amigos?

¿El clima?
¿La falta de tiempo/dinero?
¿Una enfermedad?
¿La disposición?

Comparte con tus compañeros de clase una situación reciente que viviste en la que querías hacer algo, pero algo imprevisto impidió tus planes.

_____
_____

IF/THEN CLAUSES

If I were a rich man, then I would buy an airplane.

If/then clauses express hypothetical situations and what you would do, where you would go, what you would buy, what you would eat, etc. in those situations.
- if you could…
- if you had time…
- if it were possible…
- if someone invited you…
- etc.

NOTE: In Spanish, "si" (meaning "if") is NOT the same as "sí" (meaning "yes").

CLÁUSULAS DE "SI… ENTONCES"

Si fuera un hombre rico, entonces compraría un avión.

Las clausulas "si" expresan situaciones hipotéticas y lo que harías, adónde irías, lo que comprarías, que comerías, etc. en esas situaciones.

- si pudieras…
- si tuvieras el tiempo…
- si fuera posible…
- si alguien te invitara…
- etc.

TIPS FOR LIFE

"If you're not making mistakes, then you're not doing anything." –John Wooden

CLAVES PARA LA VIDA

"Si no estás cometiendo errores, no estás haciendo nada." – John Wooden

*Now, write your own **If/then** sentences below.*

If _____,

then _____.

If _____,

then _____.

If _____,

then _____.

If _____,

then _____.

If _____,

then _____.

If _____,

then _____.

If _____,

then _____.

What are some of the interesting or crazy situations that you came up with?

*Ahora, escribe tus propias frases de "**si…entonces**" abajo.*

Si _____,

entonces _____.

Si _____,

entonces _____.

Si _____,

entonces _____.

Si _____,

entonces _____.

Si _____,

entonces _____.

Si _____,

entonces _____.

Si _____,

entonces _____.

¿Cuáles son unas situaciones interesantes o locas que inventaron?

HOMEWORK

1. Write three new sentences using **but** to express interrupted plans.
2. Write three new **if…then** sentences.

TAREA

1. Escribe tres nuevas oraciones usando **pero** para expresar planes interrumpidos.
2. Escribe tres nuevas frases con la cláusula **si… entonces.**

English

Español

LESSON 1: SIMPLE PAST TENSE
LECCION 1: PASADO SIMPLE (PRETÉRITO)

English

Español

English

Español

LESSON OBJECTIVE

Learn and practice the uses of the present perfect tense

OBJETIVO DE LA LECCIÓN

Aprender y practicar los usos del presente perfecto

VOCABULARY

1. I have eaten
2. I have been here
3. She hasn't gotten here yet.
4. I have done the following activities
5. I have been on the roller coaster
6. I have driven
7. I have fallen
8. I have eaten
9. We have seen
10. We haven't been to the Pendulum
11. We haven't ridden the slides

12. We haven't seen the city
13. We haven't been on
14. She hasn't driven
15. She hasn't eaten
16. I have seen
17. They haven't been
18. We haven't gotten dizzy

VOCABULARIO

1. (Yo) **he** com**ido**
2. He est**ado** aquí
3. Ella no ha lleg**ado** todavía.
4. He hecho las siguientes actividades
5. He est**ado** en la montaña rusa
6. He manej**ado**
7. Me he ca**ído**
8. He com**ido**
9. Hemos visto
10. No hemos ido al Péndulo.

11. No nos hemos montado en los deslizaderos
12. No hemos visto la ciudad
13. No hemos estado en
14. Ella no ha manejado
15. Ella no ha comido
16. Yo los he visto
17. Ellos no han estado
18. No nos hemos mareado

PRESENT PERFECT

Subject + *have/has* + past participle
Subject + *haven't/hasn't* + past participle

Examples:
I have visited Mexico.
She has danced salsa for 10 years.
We haven't finished dinner.

The past participle of the verb is often the same as its regular past tense form, adding **-ed** to the end (examples: dance → danc**ed**; call → call**ed**).

However, certain verbs have irregular past participles. Here are a few examples:

Verb	Simple Past	Past Participle
to be	was/were	been
to eat	ate	eaten
to get	got	gotten
to give	gave	given
to go	went	gone
to see	saw	seen
to take	took	taken

PRESENTE PERFECTO

Sujeto + *haber* + participio del pasado
Sujeto + *no haber* + participio del pasado

Ejemplos:
Yo he visitado México.
Ella ha bailado salsa.
Nosotros no hemos terminado la cena.

El verbo haber:

yo **he**	nosotros
tú **has**	**hemos**
él/ella/Ud. **ha**	vosotros
	habéis
	ellos/Uds. **han**

El participio del pasado del verbo usualmente se forma agregando las letras
-ado a los verbos -AR e **-ido** a los verbos
-ER/-IR (ejemplos: com**er** → com**ido**; bail**ar** → bail**ado**).
Sin embargo, ciertos verbos tienen participios irregulares. Unos ejemplos:

Verbo	Participio del Pasado
hacer	hecho
ver	visto
decir	dicho
poner	puesto
escribir	escrito
volver	vuelto
Estar	Estado
Llegar	Llegado

LESSON 2: PRESENT PERFECT
LECCION 2: PRESENTE PERFECTO

PRESENT PERFECT

1. Use the present perfect to talk about an action that happened before now with no specific time (today, yesterday, a month ago…).
2. You CAN use the Present Perfect with unspecific expressions such as: ever, never, once, many times, several times, before, so far, already, yet, etc.

Read the following story with different times. Pay special attention to the present perfect.

1. I am at the amusement park.
2. **I have been here** since this morning. So far I have done a lot.
3. I agreed to come with my friend Anita. **She hasn't gotten here yet**.
4. While I am waiting for her, **I have done the following activities:**
5. **I have been on the roller coaster** several times.
6. **I have driven** the tea cups twice.
7. **I have fallen** a couple of times because I have been feeling dizzy.
8. **I have eaten** a lot of candy and popcorn.
9. Now my friend Anita is here.

PRESENTE PERFECTO

1. Usa el presente perfecto para hablar de situaciones que pasaron en el pasado sin especificar el tiempo (hoy, ayer, hace un mes…)
2. PUEDES usar el presente perfecto con expresiones no específicas como: nunca, nunca más, una vez que, muchas veces, antes, hasta ahora, ya, sin embargo, etc.

Lee la siguiente historia con diferentes tiempos. Preste especial atención al presente perfecto.

1. Estoy en el parque de diversiones.
2. **He estado aquí** desde esta mañana. Hasta ahora he hecho muchas cosas.
3. Acordé venir con mi amiga Anita. **Ella no ha llegado todavía.**
4. Mientras la espero **he estado haciendo las siguientes actividades**:
5. **He estado en la montaña rusa** muchas veces.
6. **He manejado** las tazas de té dos veces.
7. **Me he caído** un par de veces porque he estado mareada.
8. **He comido** muchos dulces y palomitas de maíz.
9. Ahora mi amiga Anita está aquí.

PRESENT PERFECT	PRESENTE PERFECTO
10. Since the tea cups **we have seen** many other dizzy kids. I am glad th am not the only one. I am dizzy, embarrassed and pale.	10. Después de las tazas de té **hemos visto** muchos otros niños mareados. Me alegro de no ser la única. Estoy mareada, apenada y pálida.
11. Anita and I have so much to do:	11. Anita y yo tenemos mucho por hacer.
12. **We haven't been to the Pendulu**	12. **No hemos ido al Péndulo.**
13. **We haven't ridden the slides** at tl alpine slide.	13. **No nos hemos montado en los deslizaderos** del tobogán alpino.
14. **We haven't seen the city** from the Ferris wheel.	14. **No hemos visto la ciudad** desde la rueda de Ferris.
15. **We haven't been on** the caterpilla	15. **No hemos estado en** la oruga.
16. **She hasn't driven** the tea cups.	16. **Ella no ha manejado** las tazas de té.
17. **She hasn't eaten** popcorn or cand	17. **Ella no ha comido** palomitas de maíz y dulces.
18. The kids who are in line have been this attraction the whole day.	18. Los niños en esta fila han estado en esta atracción todo el día.
19. **I have seen** them doing this line ov and over.	19. **Yo los he visto** haciendo la fila una y otra vez.
20. They haven't done the other attractions.	20. Ellos no han estado en otras atracciones.
21. **They haven't been** in the motion simulator.	21. **Ellos no han estado** en el simulador de movimiento.
22. We haven't either.	22. Nosotras tampoco.
23. They haven't been on the Pirate Sl	23. Ellos no han estado en el barco pirata.
24. We haven't either.	24. Nosotras tampoco.
25. We haven't been on the devil's wh	25. No hemos estado en la rueda del diablo.
26. **We haven't gotten dizzy** together	26. **No nos hemos mareado** juntas.
27. We have so much to do. I am so tir So is Anita. I think we are leaving coming back tomorrow. See you tomorrow, amusement park!	27. Tenemos mucho por hacer. Estoy cansada. Anita también. Yo creo que nos vamos y regresaremos mañana. ¡Nos vemos mañana, parque de diversiones!

CLASS ACTIVITIES

What have you done today? Make a list of the things that you and your classmates have and haven't done in class today.

I have _____
You have _____
He has _____
She has _____
They have _____
You have _____
We have _____
I haven't _____
She hasn't _____
He hasn't _____
It hasn't _____
They haven't _____

ACTIVIDADES PARA LA CLASE

¿Qué has hecho hoy? Haz una lista de cosas que tú y tus compañeros de clase han o no han hecho en clase hoy.

Yo he _____
Tú has _____
Él ha _____
Ella ha _____
Ellos han_____
Ellas han_____
Nosotros hemos _____
Yo no he _____
Ella no ha _____
Él no ha _____
Esto no ha _____
Ellos no han _____

TIPS FOR LIFE

"Don't regret what you have done, regret what you should have done." -- Vincent G

CLAVES PARA LA VIDA

"No te arrepientas de lo que has hecho, arrepiéntete de lo que pudiste haber hecho." --Vincent G

HOMEWORK

Go to *Schoology* and write ten sentences describing an adventure that you have experienced.

TAREA

Ve a *Schoology* y escribe 10 oraciones describiendo una aventura que has vivido.

English	**Español**

English

Español

_____

_____

_____

_____

_____

_____

_____

_____

_____

_____

_____

_____

_____

_____

_____

LESSON 2: PRESENT PERFECT
LECCION 2: PRESENTE PERFECTO

English	Español

LESSON OBJECTIVE

Learn and practice the uses of the future tenses

OBJETIVO DE LA LECCIÓN

Aprender y practicar los usos del futuro simple

VOCABULARY

1. I will
2. You will
3. He will
4. She will
5. They will
6. I will take
7. I am going to
8. He is going to exercise
9. We are going to have dinner
10. She is going to get married
11. They are going to

VOCABULARIO

1. Yo voy a
2. Tú vas a
3. Él va a
4. Ella va a
5. Ellos van a
6. (Yo) voy a tomar
7. *(Yo) voy a*
8. Él va a hacer ejercicios
9. Nosotros vamos a cenar
10. Ella se va a casar
11. Ellos van a

TIPS FOR LIFE

"Don't underestimate the things that I will do." --Adele

CLAVES PARA LA VIDA

"Nunca subestimes las cosas que podría hacer". --Adele

FUTURE ("WILL" & "BE GOING TO")

In English, there are two ways to express the future: using *will* (negative: *won't*) or *[be] going to*. There are a few different ways to use them.

Subject + will + base verb

Subject + [to be] + going to + base verb

FUTURO (IR + A + VERBO

En español, una forma de expresar el futuro es con el verbo "ir".

Sujeto + [ir] + a + verbo infinitivo
El verbo ir:

yo **voy**	nosotros **vamos**
tú **vas**	vosotros **vais**
él/ella/Ud. **va**	ellos/Uds. **van**

FUTURE ("WILL" & "BE GOING TO")

1.   WILL: Voluntary actions or promises
I will help you with your homework.
Will you set the table?
She will take me to the airport.
I won't forget to call him.

2.   BE GOING TO: Plans
He is going to exercise more this year.
We are going to have dinner tonight.
She is going to get married in June.
You aren't going to come to the party?

3.   BOTH: Predictions
She is going to have four kids.
He will always be happy.
I am never going to get married.
They will win the Super Bowl.

Let's see how this works

1. I am going to visit my mom next summer. It is a long trip, but I don't care because we have so many plans: first, we are going to make tamales.
2. I love tamales. My mom is going to make some for me. She is going to make some with beef. She is going to make some with chicken. She will make some vegetarian. She is going to teach me. We are going to have fun. We are going to eat them all.

FUTURO (IR + A + VERBO INFINITIVO

Conjugaciones y ejemplos:

Yo voy a ir al cine esta noche.
Él va a hacer más ejercicio este año.
Ella va a tener cuatro hijos.
Tú vas a ganarte la lotería.
Nosotros vamos a hacer un largo viaje.
Ustedes van a cambiar de carrera.
Ellos se van a casar en junio.
¿No vas a ir a la fiesta?
No voy a olvidar de llamarlo.
Ella me va a llevar al aeropuerto.
Te voy a ayudar con la tarea.

Veamos cómo funciona esto:

1.   *El próximo verano voy a ir a visitar a mi mamá. Es un viaje largo, pero no me importa porque tengo muchos planes: primero vamos a hacer tamales.*

2.   *Me encantan los tamales. Mi mamá va a preparar tamales para mí. Ella va a hacer unos con carne. Ella va a hacer algunos con pollo. Ella va a hacer algunos vegetarianos. Ella me va a enseñar. Nos vamos a divertir. Nos los vamos a comer todos.*

IRREGULAR VERBS

3. She is going to knit a scarf for me. She knows that Denver is cold during the winter time so she is also going to knit gloves.

4. We are going to visit my siblings in the south of the country. I will take some medicines for them. Those are expensive and hard to find over there.

5. We will volunteer at the animal shelter. My mom likes dogs and cats and she feels sorry for the ones that people have abandoned. I am afraid that she is going to adopt one. I will help her.

6. We are going to paint my mom's apartment. She will ask her nephews for help.

7. When we finish painting, her apartment, it is going to be beautiful. She is going to love it.

8. We are going to the beach. We will sit on the seashore. We will watch the sunset. We will sit silently. We will observe carefully.

Or we will smile and talk. Or we will run and play. We will smell the soft breeze of the ocean. We will feel the breeze touching our skins.

IRREGULAR VERBS

3. Ella va a tejer una bufanda para mí. Ella sabe que Denver es frío durante el invierno, así que ella va a tejer guantes también.

4. Vamos a visitar a mis hermanos en el sur del país. Llevaré algunas medicinas para ellos. Éstas son costosas y difíciles de encontrar allá.

5. Vamos a ir como voluntarias al refugio de animales. A mi mamá le gustan los perros y los gatos y ella siente lástima por aquellos que la gente ha abandonado. Me temo que mi mamá va adoptar uno. Yo la voy a ayudar.

6. Vamos a pintar el apartamento de mi mamá. Ella le pedirá ayuda a sus sobrinos.

7. Cuando terminemos de pintar, su apartamento se va a ver muy bonito. A ella le va a encantar.

8. Vamos a ir a la playa. Nos vamos a sentar en la orilla de la playa. Veremos el atardecer. Nos vamos a sentar silenciosamente. Vamos a observar cuidadosamente.
O vamos a reír y hablar. O vamos a correr y jugar. Vamos a oler la briza suave del océano. Vamos a sentir la briza tocar nuestra piel.

IRREGULAR VERBS

9.   We will definitely enjoy the sunset.

10.   We will eat a lot of seafood. I won't drink anything other than coconut water. I won't sleep a lot. I won't fight. I won't argue. I won't cry. I won't be sad. I won't be mad. Instead I will laugh like crazy. I will jump and run. I will do everything that makes me happy. I will enjoy every minute.

11.   What will you do on your next vacation?

12.   What won't you do?

IRREGULAR VERBS

9.   Nosotras, definitivamente, vamos a disfrutar el atardecer.

10.   (Nosotras) vamos a comer mucha comida de mar. Yo no voy a tomar nada diferente de agua de coco. No voy a dormir demasiado. No voy a pelear. No voy a discutir. No voy a llorar. No voy a estar triste. No me voy a molestar. Más bien voy a reír como loca. Voy a saltar y correr. Y voy a hacer todo lo que me haga feliz. Voy a disfrutar cada minuto.

11.   ¿Qué vas a hacer (tú) en tus próximas vacaciones?

12.   ¿Qué no vas a hacer?

CLASS ACTIVITY

1.   Make a list of promises or voluntary actions (use will/won't…)

_____

_____

_____

_____

2.   Write down 5 sentences expressing plans for the next month or summer (use "be going to").

_____

_____

_____

_____

ACTIVIDAD PARA LA CLASE

1.   Haz una lista de promesas o acciones voluntarias (use voy a …/no voy a …)

_____

_____

_____

_____

2.   Escribe 5 oraciones expresando planes para el próximo mes o para el verano. (usa voy a…, va a…, vamos a…, van a …, etc)

_____

_____

_____

_____

CLASS ACTIVITY

3.   Make a list of predictions (use either *"will"* or *"be going to"*).

_____

_____

_____

_____

_____

_____

CLASS ACTIVITY

3.   Haz una lista de predicciones (usa usa voy a…, va a…, vamos a…, etc)

_____

_____

_____

_____

_____

_____

HOMEWORK

Complete the sentences using "will" or "going to…" according to the context. Review with your partner.

1. I _____ doctor next week.
2. She _____ graduate in June next year.
3. They _____ visit the shelter. They want to adopt a dog.
4. I _____ lose weight to wear a bikini during the summer.
5. When I get married _____ to a honeymoon in Fiji.
6. I _____ help my roommate with homework for school.

TAREA

Completa las oraciones haciendo tus propios planes. (usa "ir a" en todas sus conjugaciones).

1. Yo _____ al doctor la próxima semana.
2. Ella _____ graduar en junio del próximo año.
3. Ellos _____ visitar el refugio de animales.
4. Yo _____ perder peso para usar un bikini durante el verano.
5. Cuando (yo) me case _____ de luna de miel a Fiji.
6. Yo _____ ayudar a mi compañero de apartamento con su tarea para la escuela.

English

Español

_____

_____

_____

_____

_____

_____

_____

_____

_____

_____

_____

_____

_____

_____

LESSON 3: FUTURE ("WILL" AND "BE GOING TO")
LECCION 3: (IR + A + VERBO INFINITIVO)

English	Español

English

Español

_____ | _____

_____ | _____

_____ | _____

_____ | _____

_____ | _____

_____ | _____

_____ | _____

_____ | _____

_____ | _____

_____ | _____

_____ | _____

_____ | _____

_____ | _____

_____ | _____

_____ | _____

LESSON OBJECTIVE

Learn and practice the uses of the past progressive tense

OBJETIVO DE LA LECCIÓN

Aprender y practicar los usos del pasado progresivo

VOCABULARY

1. When I was
2. When we were arriving

3. While I was visiting
4. As long as
5. When I was boarding
6. Was staring at me
7. They were asking
8. Then
9. Last week
10. Last night you were
11. In that moment / At that time I was
12. At noon
13. At midnight
14. Suspicious

VOCABULARIO

1. Cuando (yo) estaba
2. Cuando (nosotros) estábamos llegando
3. Mientras estaba visitando
4. Siempre y cuando
5. Cuando estaba abordando
6. Me estaba mirando
7. Me estaban haciendo
8. Entonces
9. La semana pasada estábamos
10. Anoche estabas
11. En ese momento

12. Al mediodía
13. A la medianoche
14. Sospechosa

TIPS FOR LIFE

"I can't change the direction of the wind, but I can adjust my sails to always reach my destination".
Jimmi Dean

CLAVES PARA LA VIDA

"No puedo cambiar la dirección del viento, pero puedo ajustar mis velas para siempre lograr mi destino".
Jimmi Dean

PAST PROGRESSIVE
(PAST CONTINUOUS)

Subject + was/were + present participle

The present participle is formed by adding **-ing** to the end of the base verb. (*Examples:* walking, eating, playing)

Exceptions:
Drop the final -e on a verb before adding
-ing (but verbs ending in -ee are unchanged)
come → coming
dance → dancing
agree → agreeing
Double the final consonant of CVC verbs
sit → sitting
swim → swimming
put → putting
Final -ie becomes -y
lie → lying

PASADO PROGRESIVO
(PASADO CONTINUO)

Sujeto + [estar] + participio del presente

El participio del presente se forma agregando **-ando** a los verbos **-AR** e **-IENDO** a los verbos **-ER/-IR**. (*Ejemplos:* caminando, comiendo, jugando)

Excepción:
El participio del presente del verbo "ir" es "yendo".
El verbo estar (en pasado):

yo **estaba**   nosotros **estábamos**
tú **estabas**   vosotros **estabais**
él/ella/Ud. **estaba**   ellos/Uds. **estaban**

HOW WAS YOUR TRIP?

Mike: Hi Kathy, thanks for picking me up at the airport.
Kathy: You're welcome Mike, but tell me ... how was your trip?

¿CÓMO ESTUVO TU VIAJE?

Mike: Hola Kathy, gracias por recogerme en el aeropuerto.
Kathy: De nada Mike, pero cuéntame… ¿Cómo estuvo tu viaje?

HOW WAS YOUR TRIP?

Mike: It was awesome, I got to visit many amazing places **while I was visiting** my girlfriend in Europe.

Kathy: Good for you! Over here the weather was crazy last week while on vacation.

Mike: Yes, I know. My flight was delayed due to weather. In fact, since I left the hotel, until the plane landed I had many mishaps.

Kathy: What happened? Tell me everything.

Mike: Can you believe that **when we were arriving** at the airport a cab crashed into our car?

Kathy: I don't believe it. Was it serious? I would say you were late to your flight because of that.

Mike: No, nothing serious happened, but we were very scared. So much that **when I was boarding** the plane, I was still shaking and nervous.

Kathy: As long as nothing serious happened to anyone, everything is fine. Relax, you are here already.

¿CÓMO ESTUVO TU VIAJE?

Mike: Estuvo maravilloso; pude visitar muchos lugares increíbles **mientras estuve visitando** a mi novia en Europa.

Kathy: ¡Me alegro por ti! Acá el clima estuvo muy loco la semana pasada, durante las vacaciones.

Mike: Sí, lo sé. Mi vuelo se retrasó debido al clima. De hecho, desde que salí del hotel hasta que aterrizamos tuve muchas calamidades.

Kathy: ¿Qué te pasó? Cuéntamelo todo.

Mike:¿Puedes creer que **cuando estábamos llegando** al aeropuerto un taxi chocó nuestro carro?

Kathy: ¡No lo creo! ¿Les pasó algo grave? Me imagino que llegaste tarde a tu vuelo debido a eso.

Mike: No, nada grave, pero estábamos muy asustados. Tanto que **cuando (yo) estaba abordando** el avión, yo seguía temblando y nervioso.

Kathy: Siempre y cuando a nadie le haya pasado nada grave, todo está bien. Relájate ya estás aquí.

HOW WAS YOUR TRIP?

Mike: Wait, I have not told you everything yet. At that time, one of the flight attendants **was staring at me** and suddenly she called the police. She said that my attitude seemed suspicious.

Kathy: Are you serious? You're making up everything! Don't tell me that they arrested you.

Mike: No, it wasn't that bad. But they checked me, and **they were asking** a lot of questions while all the other passengers were boarding.

Kathy: How crazy! I guess everyone saw you as if you had a bomb.

Mike: Yes, it was a very awkward situation. But as you say, I am here. Now you tell me... how was your week off?

Have you ever experienced an awkward situation? Tell your partner an awkward story that have happened to you or come up with one. (use past progressive).

¿CÓMO ESTUVO TU VIAJE?

Mike: Espera, no te he contado todo todavía. En ese momento, una de las azafatas me estaba mirando fijamente y de pronto llamó a la policía. Dijo que mi actitud le pareció sospechosa.

Kathy: ¿Es en serio? ¡Te lo estás inventando todo! No me digas que te llevaron detenido.

Mike: No, tampoco fue para tanto. Pero sí me revisaron y (ellos) me estaban haciendo muchas preguntas mientras todos los demás pasajeros estaban abordando.

Kathy: ¡Qué loco! Me imagino que todos te veían como si trajeras una bomba.

Mike: Sí, fue una situación muy incómoda. Pero como tú dices, ya estoy acá. Ahora tú cuéntame… ¿cómo estuvo tu semana de vacaciones?

¿Alguna vez has vivido una situación incómoda? Cuéntale a tu compañero una historia incomoda que hayas vivido o invéntate una. (Usa el pasado continuo).

CLASS ACTIVITIES

Write a short story in "past progressive" tense, using words or phrases from the vocabulary.
I was walking when…

_____
_____
_____
_____
_____
_____
_____
_____
_____
_____
_____
_____
_____
_____
_____
_____
_____

ACTIVIDADES PARA LA CLASE

Escribe una corta historia en "pasado continuo" usando las palabras o frases del vocabulario.
Yo estaba caminando cuando…

_____
_____
_____
_____
_____
_____
_____
_____
_____
_____
_____
_____
_____
_____
_____
_____
_____

HOMEWORK

Write 5 sentences in "past progressive" tense, using words or phrases from the vocabulary.

TAREA

Escribe 5 oraciones en "pasado continuo" usando las palabras o frases del vocabulario.

English	Español

English

Español

ShareLingo

English

Español

_____

_____

_____

_____

_____

_____

_____

_____

_____

_____

_____

_____

_____

_____

_____

_____

LESSON OBJECTIVE

Learn and practice the uses of the future perfect tense

OBJETIVO DE LA LECCIÓN

Aprender y practicar los usos del futuro perfecto

VOCABULARY

1. I will have eaten
2. I will have applied
3. I will have visited
4. I will have learned
5. He will have gotten
6. She will have earned

VOCABULARIO

1. . (yo) Habré comido
2. Habré aplicado
3. Habré visitado
4. Habré aprendido
5. Él habrá entrado
6. Ella habrá recibido

LESSON 5: FUTURE PERFECT
LECCIÓN 5: FUTURO PERFECTO

FUTURE PERFECT

Subject + will have + past participle
Subject + won't have + past participle

Examples:
I will have eaten cake.
I will have visited my grandmother.
You will have learned English.
She will have eaten a lot today.
We won't have studied much.
He won't have liked that dessert.

Use the present perfect to talk about an action that will happen in the future before a different action takes place also in the future.
You CAN use the future perfect with time expressions such as:
- by the time
- by June of next year
- by March
- by our next anniversary
- by next week
- at this time tomorrow
- *etc.*

Read the story and pay special attention to the uses of future perfect.

8.   Planning your future is very important in the American culture. Planning everything means organizing our future.

FUTURO PERFECTO

Sujeto + [haber] + participio del pasado
El verbo haber (en futuro):
yo **habré**   nosotros **habremos**
tú **habrás**   vosotros **habréis**
él/ella/Ud. **habrá**   ellos/Uds. **habrán**
Ejemplos:
Yo h**abré** com**ido** pastel.
Yo habré visitado a mi abuela.
Tú habrás aprendido español.
Ella habrá comido mucho hoy.
No habremos estudiado mucho.

Usa el futuro perfecto para hablar de una situación que va a pasar en el futuro y antes de otra acción también en el futuro.
Se puede usar el futuro perfecto con expresiones de tiempo como:
- para cuando
- para junio del próximo año
- para marzo
- para nuestro próximo aniversario
- para la próxima semana
- a esta hora mañana
- *etc.*

Lee la siguiente historia y presta especial atención a los usos del futuro perfecto.

1. Planear el futuro es muy importante en la cultura americana. Planear todo significa organizar nuestro futuro.

FUTURE PERFECT

2. I am 15 years old and this is how I can see my future.
3. I am studying. I am in High School. I am a sophomore. I am planning on graduating from high school in two years. By the time I graduate, **I will have applied** to at least 10 colleges.

4. By the end of my last year as a high school student, **I will have visited** at least three colleges.

5. By the time I get my high School diploma, **I will have learned** all I need to go to college.

6. By the time I graduate from college, I will have enrolled as a law student.
7. If I keep really focused on studying, I will have graduate from University in five years.

FUTURO PERFECTO

2. Tengo 15 años y esta es la manera en que veo mi futuro.
3. Estoy estudiando. Estoy en preparatoria. Estoy en segundo año. Estoy planeando en graduarme de la preparatoria en dos años. Para cuando me gradúe, ya **habré aplicado** al menos a 10 Universidades.
4. Para el final de mi último año como estudiante de *prepa (preparatoria)* ya **habré visitado** al menos tres universidades.
5. Para el momento en que me den mi diploma de *prepa,* ya **habré aprendido** todo lo que necesito para ir a la universidad.
6. Para cuando me gradúe de la Universidad ya me habré matriculado como estudiante de leyes.
7. Si me mantengo realmente concentrado en estudiar, me habré graduado de la universidad en 5 años

TIPS FOR LIFE

"Take control of your future by making a choice to start it right now." -- Auliq Ice

CLAVES PARA LA VIDA

"Toma control sobre tu futuro tomando la decisión de empezar ahora mismo." --Auliq Ice

FUTURE PERFECT

8. By the time I finish Law school, I will have done my internship in a big and well known law firm.

9. By the time I get my degree as a law student I will have learned all I need to know about immigration law.

10. By this time in 7 years, I will have planned my graduation ceremony.

11. So, if my best friend wants to come along, by the time we graduate from high school **he will have gotten** into medical school.

12. By the time he graduates from Medical School he will have done his internships in multiple ER departments.

13. By the time I graduate from Law School he will have saved a lot of lives.

14. By the time he graduates from Medical School, I will have helped a lot of immigrants.

15. If our friend Anita wants to come along, by the time my best friend and I graduate, **she will have earned** her degree as Psychologist.

16. By the time we become a doctor and a lawyer she will have written at least one book.

17. Oh my god, so much to do. I must start right away. It is getting late. And you? What are your plans for the next ten years?

FUTURO PERFECTO

8. Para cuando termine la escuela de leyes, ya habré hecho prácticas en una grande y conocida compañía de abogados.

9. Para cuando reciba mi diploma como estudiante de leyes ya habré aprendido todo lo que necesito saber sobre las leyes de inmigración.

10. Para este tiempo en 7 años, ya habré planeado mi ceremonia de graduación.

11. Entonces, si mi mejor amigo se quiere unir, para cuando nos graduemos de la prepa, **él habrá entrado** a la escuela de medicina.

12. Para cuando (él) se gradúe de la escuela de medicina él habrá hecho su residencia en múltiples departamentos de emergencias.

13. Para cuando me gradúe de la escuela de leyes, él habrá salvado muchas vidas.

14. Para cuando él se gradúe de la escuela de medicina, yo habré ayudado a muchos estudiantes.

15. Si nuestra amiga Anita quiere unirse, para cuando mi mejor amigo y yo nos graduemos, **ella habrá recibido** su diploma como Psicóloga.

16. Para cuando nosotros nos convirtamos en médico y abogado, ella habrá escrito al menos un libro.

17. Dios Santo, mucho por hacer. Mejor si empiezo de una vez. Ya se me está haciendo tarde. ¿y tú? ¿Cuáles son tus planes para los próximos 10 años?

CLASS ACTIVITIES

Complete the sentences and change the verbs into the correct form.

1. By this time tomorrow I

   _____ _____
   (take) my test.
2. I am studying English really hard, my goal is that by this time next year, I

   _____
   (finish) all the levels.

3. I am practicing phone conversations in English. By tomorrow night, I

   _____ (call)
   my classmate to practice.

4. My friend Amanda is pregnant. By the end of the year she

   _____ _____
   (give birth) a beautiful baby.

5. My friend Forrest wants to buy a house. Before next year he

   _____ _____
   (buy) one.

ACTIVIDADES PARA LA CLASE

Completa las oraciones y cambie los verbos en la forma correcta.

1. Para esta hora mañana, yo

   _____ _____
   (tomar) mi examen.
2. Estoy estudiando muy duro español, entonces, mi meta es que el próximo año, para este tiempo (yo) _____

   _____ (terminar) todos los niveles.
3. Estoy practicando conversaciones telefónicas en español. Para mañana en la noche (yo)

   _____
   (llamar) a mi compañero/a de clase para practicar.
4. Mi amiga Amanda está embarazada. Para el final del año, ella _____

   _____ (dar a luz) a una hermosa bebé.
5. Mi amigo Forrest quiere comprar una casa. Antes del próximo año él

   _____ _____
   (comprar) una.

LESSON 5: FUTURE PERFECT
LECCIÓN 5: FUTURO PERFECTO

HOMEWORK

Complete the sentences making your own plans.

1. By this time tomorrow I
   _____
   _____

2. Before next month he
   _____
   _____

3. By this time next year, she

   _____
   _____

TAREA

Completa las oraciones haciendo tus propios planes.

1. Para mañana a esta hora (yo)
   _____
   _____

2. Antes del próximo mes él
   _____
   _____

3. Para este tiempo el próximo año ella

   _____
   _____

English

Español

_____

_____

_____

_____

_____

_____

_____

_____

_____

_____

_____

_____

_____

_____

_____

_____

_____

_____

_____

_____

_____

_____

_____

_____

_____

_____

_____

_____

_____

_____

_____

_____

English	Español
_____	_____
_____	_____
_____	_____
_____	_____
_____	_____
_____	_____
_____	_____
_____	_____
_____	_____
_____	_____
_____	_____
_____	_____
_____	_____
_____	_____
_____	_____

English

Español

_____

_____

_____

_____

_____

_____

_____

_____

_____

_____

_____

_____

_____

_____

_____

_____

_____

_____

_____

_____

_____

_____

_____

_____

_____

_____

_____

_____

_____

_____

ShareLingo

LESSON OBJECTIVE

Learn and practice the uses of the past perfect tense

OBJETIVO DE LA LECCIÓN

Aprender y practicar los usos del pluscuamperfecto

VOCABULARY

1. I had cooked dinner.
2. My daughter had made cookies
3. My husband had done the laundry.
4. Her husband had started a new job.
5. He had written a book.

VOCABULARIO

1. Yo había preparado la cena.
2. Mi hija había preparado galletas.
3. Mi esposo había lavado la ropa.
4. Su esposo había empezado un nuevo trabajo.
5. (él) Había escrito un libro.

TIPS FOR LIFE

Wasting time is robbing oneself! (Estonian proverb)

CLAVES PARA LA VIDA

¡Desperdiciar el tiempo es robarse a sí mismo!   (Proverbio de Estonia)

PAST PERFECT (PLUPERFECT)

(The past of the past = Two or more things that happened in the past. One happened first).
Subject + had + past participle
Look at pages 10-11 for a review of past participles.

Example:
Event 1: The flight left at 1:00pm.
Event 2: I arrived at the airport at 2:00pm.
By the time I arrived at the airport, the flight **had left**.

Use **past perfect** for the event that happened **first**, and **simple past** for the event that happened **second**.
When my husband arrived home,
   I had cooked dinner.
   I had walked my dog.
   my son had done his homework.
   my daughter had made cookies.
   we had watched our favorite TV show.

PLUSCUAMPERFECTO

(Pasado del pasado = dos eventos del pasado. Una ocurre primero).
Sujeto + [haber] + participio del pasado
Revisa las páginas 10-11 para repasar las formas de los participios del pasado.
El verbo haber (en pasado):
yo **había**   nosotros **habíamos**
tú **habías**   vosotros **habíais**
él/ella/Ud. **había**   ellos/Uds. **Habían**
Ejemplo:
Evento 1: El vuelo salió a la 1:00pm.
Evento 2: Llegué al aeropuerto a las 2pm.
Cuando llegué al aeropuerto, el vuelo **había salido**.

Usa el **pluscuamperfecto** para el evento que ocurrió **primero**, y el **pretérito simple** para el **segundo**.
Cuando mi esposo llegó a casa,
   yo había preparado la cena.
   yo había caminado a mi perro.
   mi hijo había hecho su tarea.
   mi hija había preparado galletas.
   nosotros habíamos visto nuestro programa favorito.

LESSON 6: PAST PERFECT (PLUPERFECT)
LECCIÓN 6: PLUSCUAMPERFECTO
(PASADO PERFECTO)

PAST PERFECT (PLUPERFECT)

Yesterday, by the time dinner was ready,

my husband had done the laundry.
my daughter had cleaned her room.
my youngest daughter had been to her soccer practice.
my son had picked up all of the leaves from the backyard.

By the time I finished cleaning,

my dog had left footprints all over the floor.
my toddler had emptied all the clothes from the drawers.
my son had asked for dinner three times.
my baby had gone to sleep.

By the time Alejandro retired;

He had managed a big marketing company.
He had written a book.
He had married twice.
He had made a lot of money.

PLUSCUAMPERFECTO

Ayer, para cuando la cena estuvo lista,

mi esposo había lavado la ropa.

mi hija había limpiado su habitación.
mi hija menor había ido a su práctica de futbol.
mi hijo había recogido todas las hojas del patio trasero.

Para cuando terminé de limpiar la casa;

mi perro había dejado todas las huellas en el piso.
mi bebé había sacado toda la ropa de los cajones.
mi hijo había pedido la cena 3 veces.
mi otro bebé se había ido a dormir.

Para cuando Alejandro se pensionó;

él había manejado una compañía de mercadeo grande.
(él) había escrito un libro.
(él) se había casado.
(él) había ganado mucho dinero.

PAST PERFECT (PLUPERFECT)

By the time I came to this country;
I had worked in several places.

I had lived in Mexico for many years.
I had married a great person.

When I woke up this morning;
My neighbor had cleaned his garage.
My wife had made breakfast.

My cousin had fixed the car.

My dog and cat had fought with each other many times.
My grandma had made cookies.
My grandpa had mowed the yard
My nephew had broken a window with a tennis ball.

PLUSCUAMPERFECTO

Para cuando vine a este país;
(yo) había trabajado en varios lugares.
había vivido en México por muchos años.
(yo) me había casado con una gran persona.

Cuando me desperté esta mañana;
mi vecino había limpiado su garaje.
mi esposa había hecho desayuno.
mi sobrino había reparado el carro.
mi perro y gato habían peleado entre ellos muchas veces.
mi abuela había hecho galletas.
mi abuelo había cortado el césped.
mi sobrino había roto la ventana con una pelota de tenis.

CLASS ACTIVITIES

Use the following images (both sides of the page) to create a story using past perfect. Write a letter to your partner describing what happened.

ACTIVIDADES PARA LA CLASE

Usa las siguientes imágenes (en ambos lados de la página) para crear una historia usando el Pluscuamperfecto. Escribe una carta a tu compañero describiendo que pasó.

ShareLingo

CLASS ACTIVITIES

Hi _____, How are you? I'm not so good. Last weekend was a disaster. By the time _____

_____

_____

_____

_____

_____

_____

_____

_____

CLASS ACTIVITIES

Hola _____, ¿cómo estás? Yo no muy bien. El fin de semana pasado fue un desastre. Para cuando

_____

_____

_____

_____

_____

_____

_____

_____

HOMEWORK

Call your class mate and tell him/her about your week/weekend using past perfect. Tell your experience to the rest of the class.

TAREA

Llama a tu compañero y cuéntale acerca de tu semana/fin de semana usando el pluscuamperfecto. Cuéntale tu experiencia al resto de la clase.

English

Español

English

Español

LESSON 6: PAST PERFECT (PL UPERFECT)
LECCIÓN 6: PLUSCUAMPERFECTO (PASADO PERFECTO)

English	Español

LESSON 7: PHRASAL VERBS
LECCIÓN 7: FRASES VERBALES

LESSON OBJECTIVE

Common English phrasal verbs and their uses in Spanish

OBJETIVO DE LA LECCIÓN

Algunas frases verbales que son comunes en inglés y sus usos en

VOCABULARY

1. Found out
2. Looking forward to
3. Gave in
4. Give up
5. Taking up
6. Catch up
7. Drop in
8. Pick him up
9. Stood him up
10. Take away

VOCABULARIO

1. Supo
2. Anhelando
3. Se dio por vencido
4. Abandonar
5. Empezar
6. Ponerse al día
7. Llegará
8. Lo recogiera
9. Lo dejó plantado
10. Sacar

STORY

1. Sussy <u>found out</u> that the circus was in town and has been <u>looking forward to</u> going all week. She asked Jose several times to go with her and he finally <u>gave in</u>. Good thing. Sussy was getting tired of reminding Jose and was about to <u>give up</u>.

2. Jose was excited. He had always thought about <u>taking up</u> a career in the circus.

3. There was just one problem. Jose was behind on his work so he had to <u>catch up</u> before he could go. He worked for a while and then <u>gave up.</u> Now he was ready for Sussy to <u>drop in</u> and <u>pick</u> him <u>up</u>.

4. He waited and waited but Sussy never came. She had <u>stood</u> him <u>up</u>.

5. It <u>turns out</u> that Sussy's motorcycle was very old. It had finally <u>given out</u> on the way there. She couldn't get to Jose's house and wasn't able to call him. Everybody was disappointed.

What can we <u>take away</u> from this story?

Create your own sentences using the previews phrasal verbs.

HISTORIA

1. Sussy <u>supo</u> que el circo estaba en el área y ha estado <u>anhelando</u> ir toda la semana. Le pidió a José varias veces que la acompañara hasta que él por fin <u>se dio por vencido.</u> Menos mal. Sussy se estaba cansando de recordarle a José y estaba a punto de <u>abandonar</u> la idea.

2. José estaba emocionado. Siempre había pensado en <u>empezar</u> una carrera en el circo.

3. Sólo había un problema. José estaba atrasado en su trabajo, entonces, para poder ir tuvo que <u>ponerse al día</u>. Trabajó por un ratito y por último <u>abandonó</u> su tarea. Ahora estaba listo para que Sussy <u>llegara y lo recogiera</u>.

4. Él esperó y esperó, pero Sussy nunca vino. Lo había <u>dejado plantado</u> (a él).

5. <u>Resulta</u> ser que la motocicleta de Sussy era muy vieja y por fin se <u>echó a perder</u> en el camino. No pudo llegar a la casa de José y tampoco podía comunicarse con él. Todos estaban desilusionados.

¿Qué podemos sacar de esta historia?

Crea tus propias oraciones usando las frases verbales anteriores.

SENTENCES

1. You shouldn't give up. Tough times end but resilient people keep going.
2. It is always fun to find out new facts about things that interest you.
3. I was really upset about losing my bracelet but I finally got over it.
4. Keep up the good work.
5. He has been thinking about taking up a new hobby. What do you think about scuba diving?
6. Steve is a lot further along in the project than I am. I need to catch up.
7. Did you use up all of the tooth paste today?
8. Suze stood up Carl for their first date.
9. You shouldn't talk about movies before friends have seen them. You don't want to give away the ending.
10. Matt borrowed the necklace but he gave it back to his friend.
11. I was fighting the urge to eat the cookie but I finally gave in.
12. My car lasted almost half a million miles but it finally gave out.

FRASES

1. No deberías renunciar. Los tiempos duros se acaban, pero la gente resistente sigue.
2. Siempre es divertido llegar a saber nuevos hechos acerca de las cosas que te interesan.
3. Me molestó mucho que se me perdió la pulsera, pero por fin ya lo superé.
4. ¡Mantén el buen trabajo!
5. Él ha estado pensando en tomar un hobby nuevo. ¿Qué piensas de bucear?
6. Steve se encuentra más avanzado en el proyecto que yo. Necesito ponerme al día.
7. ¿Usaste/acabaste toda la pasta dental hoy?
8. Suze dejó plantado a Carl para su primera cita.
9. No deberían hablar de las películas antes de que los amigos las hayan visto. No quieres revelar el final.
10. Matt pidió prestado el collar, pero se lo devolvió a su amigo.
11. Yo estaba luchando contra las ganas de comerme la galleta, pero al final me di por vencido.
12. Mi coche alcanzó casi medio millón de -millas, pero al final se echó a perder.

SENTENCES

13. What are you <u>giving up</u> for lent?

14. If I don't wash my face every day, my face will <u>break out</u>.

15. She has been <u>looking forward to</u> going to the circus all week.

16. I think that was a really good lesson. What did you <u>take away</u> from it?

17. Can someone <u>drop</u> you <u>off</u> at the theater?

18. The class turned out to be really hard for Jose. He had to <u>drop out</u>.

19. Carlos said that I could <u>drop in at</u> any time I want.

FRASES

13. ¿Qué cosa <u>dejarás</u> por la cuaresma?

14. Si no me lavo la cara todos los días, me <u>saldrán</u> imperfecciones.

15. Ella ha estado <u>esperando con expectativa</u> ir al circo toda la semana.

16. Creo que fue una lección muy buena. ¿Qué <u>sacaste</u> de ella?

17. ¿Puede alguien <u>ir a dejar</u>te en el cine?

18. La clase resultó ser muy difícil para José. Tuvo de <u>dejarla</u>.

19. Carlos me dijo que yo podría <u>hacer una parada</u> en cualquier momento que quisiera.

CLASS ACTIVITIES

Read the phrases and match the appropriate phrasal verb to each and then rewrite the sentence using the phrasal verb.

1. Something was really important to me but now it's not so much.

   _____

2. I have a lot of work to do. I should do everything that I need to.

ACTIVIDADES PARA LA CLASE

Lee las frases y escribe la frase verbal adecuada en el espacio. Luego redacta la frase nuevamente usando el verbo nuevo.

1. Antiguamente algo era muy importante para mí, pero hoy en día no tanto.

   _____

2. Tengo mucho trabajo que hacer. Debo hacer todo lo que necesito.

   _____

CLASS ACTIVITIES

3. Jim had something of Martha's. Now Martha has it again.

    _____

4. I missed not having the amusement park open in the Winter. I know I'll be really happy this Spring when it opens up again.

    _____

5. Bill will take you to the show and leave you there.

    _____

6. Mario didn't know much about sharks but he read a book and then knew that they have sharp teeth.

    _____

7. I was running for a very long time. Finally, I couldn't go any longer.

    _____

8. Sometimes Maria comes to visit me at work. It's not a planned appointment.

    _____

Answers:
1. Catch up. I need to catch up.

2. Give back. He gave it back.
3. Look forward to. I look forward to it.

ACTIVIDADES PARA LA CLASE

3. Jim tenía algo que pertenecía a Marta. Ahora ella lo tiene nuevamente.

    _____

4. Eché de menos no tener el parque de diversiones abierto durante el invierno. Estaré muy feliz cuando abra de nuevo en la primavera.

    _____

5. Bill te llevará al evento y te dejará allí.

    _____

6. Mario no sabía mucho a cerca de los tiburones, pero leyó un libro y después sabía que tienen los dientes muy afilados.

    _____

7. Yo corrí por mucho tiempo y por fin me agoté demasiado, no pude continuar.

    _____

8. A veces María viene a visitarme en el trabajo. No es una cita programada.

    _____

Respuestas:
1. Ponerse al día. Necesito ponerme al día.
2. Devolver. Se lo devolvió.
3. Esperar con anticipación. Espero con anticipación.

CLASS ACTIVITIES

4. Drop off. He'll drop you off.
5. Find out. He found out about sharks.
6. Give out. I gave out.

7. Drop in. She drops in.

ACTIVIDADES PARA LA CLASE

4. Dejar. Te dejará.
5. Saber (en el pasado). Él supo de los tiburones.
6. No poder más. No pude más. *(Cuando se trata de personas, se usa "no poder" y no "echarse a perder")*
7. Llegar. Llega a la oficina.

TIPS FOR LIFE

"Genius is one percent inspiration and 99 percent perspiration,"

Thomas Edison.

CLAVES PARA LA VIDA

"Un genio es uno por ciento de inspiración y 99 por ciento de sudoración".

Thomas Edison.

HOMEWORK

Write five sentences using phrasal verbs.
Think of a fun story to remember one of the difficult phrasal verb and its meaning. Share it with the class.

TAREA

Escribe 5 oraciones con los verbos compuestos.
Piensa en una historia divertida para ayudarte acordar de un verbo compuesto y su significado. Compártelo con la clase.

English	Español

English

Español

English

Español

_____   _____

_____   _____

_____   _____

_____   _____

_____   _____

_____   _____

_____   _____

_____   _____

_____   _____

_____   _____

_____   _____

_____   _____

_____   _____

_____   _____

_____   _____

SHARELINGO
Connecting Cultures Through Language

LESSON OBJECTIVE

Learn how to make sentences in the passive and active voices

OBJETIVO DE LA LECCIÓN

Aprender a elaborar oraciones en voz pasiva y voz activa

VOCABULARY

1. Was written
2. Unpublished
3. Was recommended
4. Eclipse
5. Release
6. Satisfied
7. Has/Have been
8. Lucky
9. Autographed
10. Emphasize

VOCABULARIO

1. Fue escrito
2. Inéditas
3. Fue recomendado
4. Eclipse
5. Lanzamiento
6. Satisfecha
7. Ha/Han Sido
8. Afortunados
9. Autografiadas
10. Enfatizar

PASSIVE VOICE & ACTIVE VOICE

The **active voice** is used to emphasize who or what is performing the action.
Ex: *The President of Japan* <u>recommended</u> the book.
The **passive voice** is used to emphasize the action itself. Often the subject of the action does not even appear.
Ex: *The book* <u>was recommended</u> by the President of Japan.

VOZ PASIVA & VOZ ACTIVA

La **voz activa** se usa para enfatizar a quién o qué está realizando la acción.

Ej: *El Presidente de Japón* <u>recomendó</u> el libro.
La **voz pasiva** se usa para enfatizar la acción en sí. A menudo el sujeto de la acción ni siquiera aparece.

Ej: *El libro* <u>fue recomendado</u> por el Presidente de Japón.

PRESENTATION OF A BOOK

1. The famous Chilean writer, Nadia Bolívar, **presents** her latest achievement. The book <u>was written</u> last year, during her trip to Japan. The work **talks about** the many experiences, that the author had in the Asian country. Also, several unpublished photographs **are collected** in the book.
2. The author said that she was satisfied with her book. The most renowned newspapers **have written** good reviews about her it. Surprisingly, the book <u>was recommended</u> by the President of Japan himself.

LANZAMIENTO DE UN LIBRO

1. La famosa escritora chilena, Nadia Bolívar, **nos presenta** su último éxito. El libro <u>fue escrito</u> el año pasado, durante su viaje a Japón. La obra **cuenta** las numerosas vivencias que la autora tuvo en el país asiático. Varias fotografías inéditas también <u>son recopiladas</u> en el libro.
2. La autora dijo sentirse satisfecha con su libro. Los más destacados diarios le **han escrito** buenas críticas a su trabajo. Sorprendentemente, el libro <u>fue recomendado</u> por el mismísimo Presidente de Japón.

PRESENTATION OF A BOOK

3. Surely, the bookstores around the world will be filled with people interested in buying the book. Thousands of copies have been autographed by the author, as a surprise for her readers.

4. We recommend you to visit your favorite bookstore. Without any doubt, the book will be sold like hotcakes. Who knows, you could be one, of the lucky ones, who gets an autographed copy of the book.

LANZAMIENTO DE UN LIBRO

3. Seguramente, las librerías de todo el mundo estarán repletas con gente interesada en comprar el libro. Miles de copias han sido autografiadas por la autora, como sorpresa para sus lectores.

4. Le recomendamos que visite su librería favorita. Sin dudar, el libro será vendido como "pan caliente". Quien sabe, usted podría ser uno de los afortunados que reciba una de las copias autografiadas.

EXAMPLES

Javier <u>completed</u> the questionnaire.
The questionnaire <u>was completed</u> by Javier.
The National Food Association <u>approves</u> this product.
This product <u>has been approved</u> by the National Food Association.

The whole world <u>will observe</u> the eclipse.
The eclipse <u>will be observed</u> by the whole world.
The students <u>recorded</u> several videos.

Several videos <u>were recorded</u> by the students.

EJEMPLOS

Javier <u>completó</u> el cuestionario.
El cuestionario <u>fue completado</u> por Javier.
La Asociación Nacional de Alimentos <u>aprueba</u> este producto.
Este producto <u>ha sido aprobado</u> por la Asociación Nacional de Alimentos.

Todo el mundo <u>observará</u> el eclipse.

El eclipse <u>será observado</u> por todo el mundo.
Los estudiantes <u>grabaron</u> varios videos.
Varios videos <u>fueron grabados</u> por los estudiantes.

EXAMPLES

I change the sheets every week.

The sheets are changed every week.

Harry ate six shrimp at dinner. (active)

At dinner, six shrimp were eaten by Harry.

The crew paved the entire stretch of highway.
The entire stretch of highway was paved by the crew.

I will clean the house every Saturday.
The house will be cleaned by me every Saturday.

Tom painted the entire house.
The entire house was painted by Tom.
The choir really enjoys that piece.
That piece is really enjoyed by the choir.

The forest fire destroyed the whole suburb.
The whole suburb was destroyed by the forest fire.

EJEMPLOS

Yo cambio las sábanas todas las semanas.
Las sábanas son cambiadas todas las semanas.

Harry comió seis camarones a la cena.
A la cena, seis camarones fueron comidos por Harry.

La tripulación pavimento todo el tramo de la carretera.
Todo el tramo de la carretera fue pavimentado por la tripulación.

Voy a limpiar la casa cada sábado.
La casa será limpiada cada sábado.

Tom pintó toda la casa.
Toda la casa fue pintada por Tom.

El coro realmente disfruto esa pieza.
Esa pieza es realmente disfrutada por el coro.

El incendio forestal destruyó todo el barrio.
Todo el barrio fue destruido por el incendio forestal.

TIPS FOR LIFE

"It is the time you have wasted for your rose that makes your rose so important".
-Antoine de Saint-Exupery

CLAVES PARA LA VIDA

"Fue el tiempo que pasaste con tu rosa lo que la hizo tan importante".
-Antoine de Saint-Exupery

CLASS ACTIVITIES

Identify in each of the paragraphs when the passive or active voice is used in a sentence. Using these examples, write new sentences.
(Active) _____
_____
(Passive) _____
_____
(Active) _____
_____
(Passive) _____
_____
(Active) _____
_____
(Passive) _____
_____

ACTIVIDADES PARA LA CLASE

Identifica en cada uno de los párrafos, cuando en la oración se utiliza la voz pasiva o activa. Usando estos ejemplos escribe nuevas oraciones.
(Activa) _____
_____
(Pasiva) _____
_____
(Activa) _____
_____
(Pasiva) _____
_____
(Activa) _____
_____
(Pasiva) _____
_____

HOMEWORK

Work with a partner in *Schoology*.

Write 5 sentences in passive voice. Now ask your partner to change them into active voice.
Change roles. Write another 5 sentences.

TAREA

Trabaja con un compañero en *Schoology*.
Escribe 5 oraciones en voz pasiva.
Ahora pídele a tu compañero que las cambie a voz activa.
Cambia roles. Escribe 5 nuevas oraciones.

English

Español

_____

_____

_____

_____

_____

_____

_____

_____

_____

_____

_____

_____

_____

English

Español

_____

_____

_____

_____

_____

_____

_____

_____

_____

_____

_____

_____

_____

_____

_____

_____

English

Español

LESSON OBJECTIVE

Listening and comprehension

OBJETIVO DE LA LECCIÓN

Escuchar y comprender

READING FOR YOUR PARTNER: INSTRUCTIONS

Read for your partner in your native language and in a natural conversation speed.
Read one paragraph at the time.
Ask your partner to translate for you what you just read.
Ask your partner for his/her opinion about the paragraph.
Correct him/her. Explain the corrections. (The corrections are about the grammatical constructions not personal opinions).
Answer the questions at the end of the doc.
Create new questions.

1. BEANS; AS LATIN AS WE ARE *(from RECIPIES & COOKING)*

Simply saying the word "bean" makes me think of Latin America. Just ask any Latino how often they eat beans in their home. I don't know about you, but in mine, they are eaten almost every day in several ways: With porridge, with *congrí* rice, and with salads. They come in so many sizes, shapes, and colors that I could never get tired of eating them. Is it the same for you?

LEER PARA TU COMPAÑERO: INSTRUCCIONES

Lee para tu compañero(a) en tu idioma nativo y en una velocidad natural de conversación.
Lee un párrafo a la vez.
Pide a tu compañero(a) que traduzca lo que acabas de leer.
Pregúntale a tu compañero(a) su opinión acerca del párrafo.
Corrige a tu compañero. Explícale la corrección. (Las correcciones son acerca de la construcción gramatical no sobre las opiniones).
Responde las preguntas al final del documento.
Crea nuevas preguntas.

1. FRIJOLES: TAN LATINOS COMO NOSOTROS *(de RECETAS Y COCINA)*

Decir frijoles, me hace pensar en Latinoamerica. Solo, pregúntale a cualquier latino con qué frecuencia comen frijoles en su casa. No sé en tu casa, pero en la mía los degustamos casi a diario de diferentes maneras: en potajes, arroz congrí, ensaladas… La verdad es que nos encantan, y como son tantas sus variedades, pues nunca nos cansamos de comerlos. ¿Acaso te pasa lo mismo?

READING FOR YOUR PARTNER: INSTRUCTIONS

2. THANKSGIVING *(from National Geographic)*

Thanksgiving Day is a national holiday celebrated primarily in the United States and Canada as a day of giving thanks for the blessing of the harvest and of the preceding year. It is celebrated on the fourth Thursday of November in the United States and on the second Monday of October in Canada.

The Celebration

One day that fall, four settlers were sent to hunt for food for a harvest celebration. The Wampanoag heard gunshots and alerted their leader, Massasoit, who thought the English might be preparing for war. Massasoit visited the English settlement with 90 of his men to see if the war rumor was true. Soon after their visit, the Native Americans realized that the English were only hunting for the harvest celebration. Massasoit sent some of his own men to hunt deer for the feast and for three days, the English and native men, women, and children ate together. The meal consisted of deer, corn, shellfish, and roasted meat, far from today's traditional Thanksgiving feast. They also played ball games, sang, and danced. Much of what most modern Americans eat on Thanksgiving was not available in 162.

LEER PARA TU COMPAÑERO: INSTRUCCIONES

2. DIA DE ACCION DE GRACIAS *(de National Geographic)*

Día de Acción de Gracias es una fiesta nacional que se celebra principalmente en Estados Unidos y Canadá como un día de dar gracias por la bendición de la cosecha del año anterior. Se celebra el cuarto jueves de noviembre en los EE.UU y el segundo lunes de octubre en Canadá.

La Celebración

Un día de otoño, cuatro colonos fueron enviados a buscar comida para una celebración de la cosecha. El Wampanoag escuchó disparos y alertó a su líder, Massasoit, que pensaban que los ingleses podrían estarse preparando para la guerra. Massasoit visitó el asentamiento inglés con 90 de sus hombres para ver si el rumor de guerra era cierto. Poco después de su visita, los nativos americanos se dieron cuenta de que el inglés sólo estaban cazando para la celebración de la cosecha. Massasoit envió a algunos de sus propios hombres para cazar ciervos para la fiesta y durante tres días, los hombres, las mujeres y los niños ingleses y nativos comieron juntos. La comida consistió en venado, maíz, mariscos y carne asada, lejos de la tradicional fiesta de Acción de Gracias de hoy. También jugaron los juegos de pelota, cantaron y bailaron. Gran parte de lo que la mayoría de los estadounidenses consumen en el Día Acción de Gracias moderno no estaba disponible en 1621.

READING FOR YOUR PARTNER: INSTRUCTIONS

In 1863 President Abraham Lincoln declared two national Thanksgivings; one in August to commemorate the Battle of Gettysburg and the other in November to give thanks for "general blessings" that the modern holiday came to be.

Native Americans and Thanksgiving

The peace between the Native Americans and settlers lasted for only a generation. The Wampanoag people do not share in the popular reverence for the traditional New England Thanksgiving. For them, the holiday is a reminder of betrayal and bloodshed. Since 1970, many native people have gathered at the statue of Massasoit in Plymouth, Massachusetts each Thanksgiving Day to remember their ancestors and the strength of the Wampanoag.

LEER PARA TU COMPAÑERO: INSTRUCCIONES

En 1863 el presidente Abraham Lincoln declaró dos Thanksgivings nacionales, uno en agosto para conmemorar la Batalla de Gettysburg y la otra en noviembre para dar gracias por " bendiciones generales".

Nativos americanos y el Día de Acción de Gracias

La paz entre los nativos americanos y los colonos duró sólo una generación. El pueblo Wampanoag no comparte la reverencia popular a la tradición de Nueva Inglaterra de Acción de Gracias. Para ellos, la fiesta es un recuerdo de la traición y el derramamiento de sangre. Desde 1970, muchas personas indígenas se han reunido en la estatua de Massasoit en Plymouth, Massachusetts cada Día de Acción de Gracias para recordar a sus antepasados y la fortaleza de los Wampanoag.

TIPS FOR LIFE

"Let go of things that you cannot change, focus on the ones you can"
Anonymous

CLAVES PARA LA VIDA

"Deja ir las cosas que no puedes cambiar, pon tu atención en las que puedes cambiar"
Anonimo

SHARELINGO

READING FOR YOUR PARTNER: INSTRUCTIONS

LEER PARA TU COMPAÑERO: INSTRUCCIONES

3. THE BILINGUAL BRAIN
Susan Perry,
http://www.brainfacts.org/ sensing-thinking-behaving/language/articles/2008/the-bilingual-brain/
Neurological scientists are learning that speaking more than one language may have cognitive benefits that extend from childhood into old age.

If you also speak Spanish (or any other language), your brain may have developed some distinct advantages over your monolingual peers. New research into the neurobiology of bilingualism has found that being fluent in two languages, particularly from early childhood, not only enhances a person's ability to concentrate, but might also protect against the onset of dementia and other age-related cognitive decline. Although scientists don't know why bilingualism creates this "cognitive reserve," some theorize that speaking two languages may increase blood and oxygen flow to the brain and keep nerve connections healthy—factors thought to help ward off dementia.

3. EL CEREBRO BILINGÜE
Susan Perry,
http://www.brainfacts.org/ sensing-thinking-behaving/language/articles/2008/the-bilingual-brain/
Los científicos neurológicos están encontrando que el hablar más de un idioma podría tener beneficios cognitivos que se extienden más allá de la niñez hasta la edad adulta.

Si hablas inglés (o algún otro idioma), tu cerebro quizás ha desarrollado algunas ventajas que lo distinguen del de tus amigos monolingües. Nuevas investigaciones en la neurobiología del bilingüismo han encontrado que el ser fluido en dos idiomas, particularmente desde una edad temprana, no solo mejora la habilidad de una persona para concentrarse, sino que también puede que lo proteja del inicio de la demencia y otros declives cognitivos relacionados con la edad.

Aunque los científicos no saben porque el bilingüismo crea esta "reserva cognitiva," algunos teorizan que hablar dos idiomas podría incrementar el flujo de sangre y oxígeno en el cerebro y mantener las conexiones nerviosas saludables – factores que se piensan ayudan a evitar la demencia.

LEER PARA TU COMPAÑERO: INSTRUCCIONES

QUESTIONS
1. Do like beans? How do you like them?
2. Do you celebrate thanksgiving?
3. What is a harvest celebration?
4. Which president declared Thanksgiving a national celebration?
5. What do you think about having Thanksgiving as a National celebration?
6. How do you feel about being bilingual?
7. Tell your partner a funny story that happened to you related to being bilingual.

LEER PARA TU COMPAÑERO: INSTRUCCIONES

PREGUNTAS
1. ¿Te gustan los frijoles? ¿Cómo los prefieres?
2. ¿Celebras el día de acción de gracias?
3. ¿Qué es la celebración de la Cosecha?
4. ¿Qué presidente declaro el día de acción de gracias como una fiesta nacional?
5. ¿Qué opinas de tener el día de acción de gracias como una fiesta nacional?
6. ¿Cómo te hace sentir el ser bilingüe?
7. Cuéntale a tu compañero una historia de algo que te pasó relacionada con ser bilingüe.

LESSON 9: LISTENING PRACTICE
LECCIÓN 9: PRÁCTICA AUDITIVA

HOMEWORK

Call your partner this week and read a short story to them. Before this class finishes agree on the best time to make the phone call and who makes the first phone call. Then talk about the story.

TAREA

Llama a tu compañero esta semana y léele una corta historia esta semana. Antes de que termine esta clase acuerden en el mejor momento para hacer la llamada y quien llama primero. Entonces hablen sobre la historia.

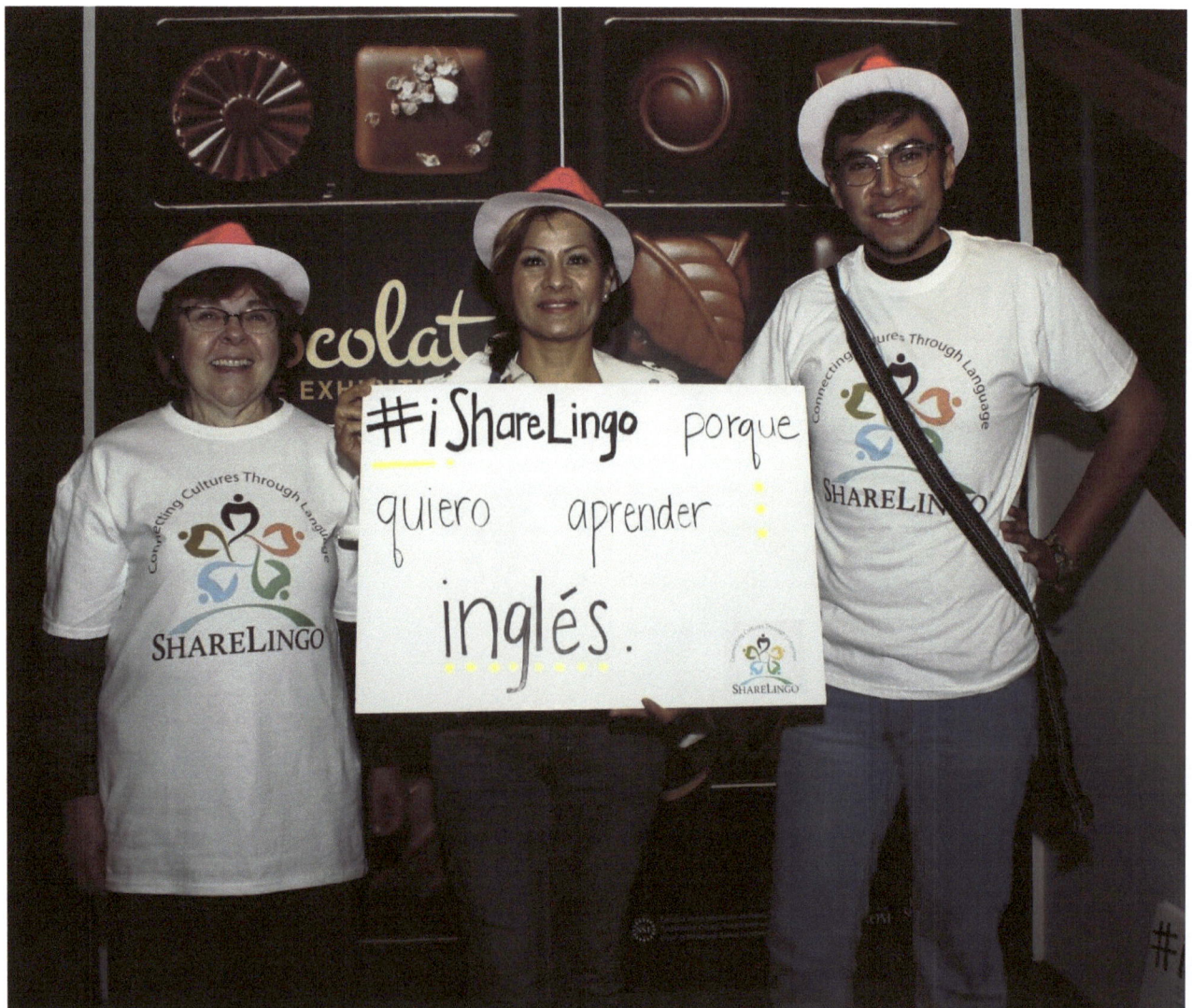

ShareLingo
Connecting Cultures Through Language

English

Español

_____

_____

_____

_____

_____

_____

_____

_____

_____

_____

_____

_____

_____

English	**Español**
_____	_____
_____	_____
_____	_____
_____	_____
_____	_____
_____	_____
_____	_____
_____	_____
_____	_____
_____	_____
_____	_____
_____	_____
_____	_____

English

Español

LESSON OBJECTIVE

Improving pronunciation

OBJETIVO DE LA LECCIÓN

Mejorar la pronunciación

KARAOKE
THE COLOR OF HOPE

1. I know what's in your eyes with just looking at you
   (I know) you're tired of walking and walking
   and walking, always in circles in the same place
2. I know that windows can be opened to change the atmosphere depends on you
   it'll help you, it's worth it once more

3. To know it's possible, to want it to happen
   to get rid of our fears, to expel them
   to paint our faces with the color of hope
   to tempt the future with our hearts
4. It's better to get lost than never having boarded
   better to fall in temptation than giving up trying
   even though you see it's not that easy to start

KARAOKE
COLOR ESPERANZA

1. Sé que hay en tus ojos con solo mirar
   que estas cansado de andar y de andar
   y caminar, girando siempre en un lugar.
2. Sé que las ventanas se pueden abrir
   cambiar el aire depende de ti
   te ayudará, vale la pena una vez mas

3. Saber que se puede, querer que se pueda
   Quitarse los miedos, sacarlos afuera
   pintarse la cara color esperanza
   tentar al futuro con el corazón

4. Es mejor perderse que nunca embarcar
   mejor tentarse a dejar de intentar
   aunque ya ves que no es tan fácil empezar

KARAOKE
THE COLOR OF HOPE

5. I know that impossible can be achieved
   that sadness will go one day
   and it'll be like that, life will change and change
6. You'll feel your soul flying
   for singing one more time
7. To know it's possible, to want it to happen
   to get rid of our fears, to expel them
   to paint our faces with the color of hope
   to tempt the future with our hearts
8. To know it's possible, to want it to happen
   to get rid of our fears, to expel them
   to paint our faces with the color of hope
   to tempt the future with our hearts
9. It's better being able to shine
   than just trying to look at the sun
10. To paint our faces with the color of hope to tempt the future with our hearts
11. To know it's possible
    to want it to happen
    To paint our faces with the color of hope
    to tempt the future with our hearts

Taken from
http://lyricstranslate.com/en/color-esperanza-diego-torres-colour-hope.html#ixzz3Jf0SqtQM

KARAOKE
COLOR ESPERANZA

5. Sé que lo imposible se puede lograr
   que la tristeza algun día se irá
   y asi será, la vida cambia y cambiará.
6. Sentirás que el alma vuela
   por cantar una vez mas
7. Saber que se puede querer que se pueda
   quitarse los miedos, sacarlos afuera
   pintarse la cara color esperanza
   tentar al futuro con el corazón
8. Saber que se puede querer que se pueda
   quitarse los miedos, sacarlos afuera
   pintarse la cara color esperanza
   tentar al futuro con el corazón
9. Vale más poder brillar que solo buscar ver el sol
10. Pintarse la cara color esperanza
    tentar al futuro con el corazón
11. Saber que se puede...
    Querer que se pueda...
    Pintarse la cara color esperanza
    tentar al futuro con el corazón

Tomado de:
http://lyricstranslate.com/en/color-esperanza-diego-torres-colour-hope.html#ixzz3Jf0W4U00

TIPS FOR LIFE

Never stop learning!

CLAVES PARA LA VIDA

¡Nunca pares de aprender!

AM I WRONG?

1. Am I wrong for thinking out the box from where I stay?
Am I wrong for saying that I'll choose another way?
I ain't trying to do what everybody else doing
Just cause everybody doing what they all do
If one thing I know, how far would I grow?
I'm walking down this road of mine, this road that I call home
2. So am I wrong for thinking that we could be something for real?
Now am I wrong for trying to reach the things that I can't see?
But that's just how I feel, that's just how I feel
That's just how I feel trying to reach the things that I can't see
3. Am I tripping for having a vision?
My prediction; I'mma be on the top of the world
Hope you, hope you don't look back, always do what you decide
Don't let them control your life, that's just how I feel
Fight for yours and don't let go, don't let them compare you, no
Don't worry, you're not alone, that's just how we feel

¿ESTOY EQUIVOCADO?

1. ¿Me equivoco por pensar fuera de la caja de donde me quedo?
¿Me equivoco por decir que elegiré otro camino?
No intento hacer lo que hacen los demás
Solo porque todo el mundo hace lo que hace
¿Si hay algo que sé, hasta dónde crecería yo?
Voy por este camino mío, a lo que llamo "hogar".
2. Entonces, ¿me equivoco por creer que podríamos ser algo en serio?
Entonces, ¿me equivoco por intentar llegar a lo que no puedo ver?
Pero así es como me siento, así es como me siento
Así es como me siento intentando llegar a lo que no puedo ver
3. ¿Me he tropezado por tener una visión?
Mi predicción, estaré en la cima del mundo
Espero, espero que no mires hacía atrás, siempre haz lo que decidas
No dejes que controlen tu vida, así es como me siento
Lucha por los tuyos y no los dejes ir, no dejes que te compraren, no
No te preocupes, no estás sola, así es como nos sentimos

AM I WRONG?

¿ESTOY EQUIVOCADO?

4. So am I wrong for thinking that we could be something for real?
Now am I wrong for trying to reach the things that I can't see?
But that's just how I feel, that's just how I feel
That's just how I feel trying to reach the things that I can't see

5. If you tell me I'm wrong, wrong
I don't wanna be right, right
If you tell me I'm wrong, wrong
I don't wanna be right

6. So am I wrong for thinking that we could be something for real?
Now am I wrong for trying to reach the things that I can't see?
But that's just how I feel, that's just how I feel
That's just how I feel trying to reach the things that I can't see

Taken from http://lyricstranslate.com/en/am-i-wrong-%C2%BFestoy-equivocado.html#ixzz3Jf0i71qm

4. Entonces, ¿me equivoco por creer que podríamos ser algo en serio?
Entonces, ¿me equivoco por intentar llegar a lo que no puedo ver?
Pero así es como me siento, así es como me siento
Así es como me siento intentando llegar a lo que no puedo ver

5. Si me dices que me equivoco, me equivoco
No quiero tener razón, razón
Si me dices que me equivoco, me equivoco
No quiero tener razón, razón

6. Entonces, ¿me equivoco por creer que podríamos ser algo en serio?
Entonces, ¿me equivoco por intentar llegar a lo que no puedo ver?
Pero así es como me siento, así es como me siento
Así es como me siento intentando llegar a lo que no puedo ver

Taken from http://lyricstranslate.com/en/am-i-wrong-%C2%BFestoy-equivocado.html#ixzz3Jf0pZ2Le

HOMEWORK

Enroll in the next class ☺

TAREA

Regístrate para la próxima clase ☺

English	Español

English	Español

English	Español

1233 Unique English Words in order of number of occurrences i.e. "i" occurs 222 times.

222 i, 85 have, 83 you, 76 will, 74 in, 71 that, 59 my, 58 we, 55 was, 53 she, 47 had, 44 going, 42 if, 40 he, 39 your, 39 time, 38 with, 36 it, 36 but, 34 at, 32 am, 30 past, 29 up, 28 what, 24 would, 24 how, 23 do, 23 from, 23 this, 22 me, 22 on, 22 they, 22 been, 22 haven't, 21 then, 21 lesson, 21 about, 20 so, 19 her, 19 were, 19 as, 19 future, 19 our, 18 perfect, 17 or, 17 one, 17 just, 16 feel, 16 know, 16 not, 16 sentences, 15 class, 15 out, 15 them, 15 go, 14 won't, 14 next, 14 book, 14 wrong, 13 now, 13 all, 13 homework, 13 done, 13 get, 13 see, 12 could, 12 write, 12 life, 12 has, 12 use, 12 when, 11 can, 11 using, 11 eaten, 11 happened, 11 story, 11 lot, 11 things, 11 some, 11 partner, 11 week, 11 school, 11 that's, 10 give, 10 objective, 10 new, 10 activities, 10 vocabulary, 10 tips, 10 hasn't, 10 take, 10 many, 10 friend, 10 something, 10 make, 10 year, 10 day, 10 tell, 10 hope, 10 it's, 10 active, 10 thanksgiving, 9 present, 9 here, 9 subject, 9 talk, 9 participle, 9 dinner, 9 verb, 9 call, 9 gave, 9 before, 9 times, 9 don't, 9 english, 9 drop, 9 change, 9 really, 9 passive, 9 voice, 9 trying, 9 want, 8 practice, 8 seen, 8 verbs, 8 several, 8 read, 8 other, 8 much, 8 who, 8 him, 8 everything, 8 his, 7 plans, 7 an, 7 eat, 7 also, 7 like, 7 uses, 7 tense, 7 gotten, 7 examples, 7 years, 7 house, 7 possible, 7 come, 7 over, 7 visit, 7 every, 7 end, 7 graduate, 7 can't, 7 reach, 7 phrasal, 7 than, 7 national, 7 color, 7 don't, 6 more, 6 right, 6 learn, 6 only, 6 action, 6 never, 6 while, 6 think, 6 tomorrow, 6 people, 6 married, 6 there, 6 two, 6 help, 6 always, 6 paint, 6 progressive, 6 last, 6 walking, 6 good, 6 into, 6 law, 6 written, 6 their, 6 finally, 6 work, 6 thinking, 6 native, 6 celebration, 5 better, 5 following, 5 dizzy, 5 pay, 5 visited, 5 today, 5 anita, 5 mom, 5 whole, 5 back, 5 airport, 5 first, 5 ask, 5 flight, 5 very, 5 off, 5 money, 5 buy, 5 happen, 5 high, 5 need, 5 doing, 5 away, 5 made, 5 look, 5 forward, 5 catch, 5 jose, 5 any, 5 president, 5 three, 5 faces, 5 tempt, 5 hearts, 4 dance, 4 no, 4 far, 4 situations, 4 express, 4 since, 4 tired, 4 same, 4 else, 4 different, 4 own, 4 phone, 4 long, 4 trip, 4 thought, 4 makes, 4 dog, 4 eggs, 4 crazy, 4 came, 4 yet, 4 left, 4 serious, 4 questions, 4 driven, 4 learned, 4 you're, 4 keep, 4 making, 4 daughter, 4 husband, 4 event, 4 each, 4 i'm, 4 found, 4 looking, 4 sussy, 4 having, 4 recommended, 4 japan, 4 world, 4 entire, 4 said, 4 language, 4 harvest, 4 massasoit, 4 americans, 4 bilingual, 4 brain, 4 being, 4 let, 4 etc, 3 often, 3 amusement, 3 park, 3 experienced, 3 where, 3 tea, 3 cups, 3 because, 3 kids, 3 spanish, 3 either, 3 together, 3 called, 3 pick, 3 list, 3 adding, 3 yes, 3 party, 3 ways, 3 base, 3 place, 3 stop, 3 june, 3 happy, 3 summer, 3 fun, 3 during, 3 country, 3 hard, 3 find, 3 ones, 3 share, 3 finish, 3 sit, 3 asked, 3 complete, 3 short, 3 boarding, 3 ate, 3 final, 3 thanks, 3 friends, 3 got, 3 car, 3 awkward, 3 phrases, 3 planning, 3 important, 3 old, 3 studying, 3 least, 3 student, 3 best, 3 wants, 3 along, 3 medical, 3 rather, 3 start, 3 taken, 3 cookies, 3 say, 3 arrived, 3 home, 3 son, 3 cleaned, 3 create, 3 weekend, 3 another, 3 taking, 3 fresh, 3 stood, 3 circus, 3 everybody, 3 giving, 3 most, 3 eclipse, 3 autographed, 3 emphasize, 3 used, 3 month, 3 author, 3 weather, 3 food, 3 beans, 3 holiday, 3 wampanoag, 3 meaning, 3 men, 3 http, 3 may, 3 cognitive, 3 situation, 3 rid, 3 fears, 3 expel, 3 danced, 3 real, 2 told, 2 tamales, 2 love, 2 knit, 2 knows, 2 winter, 2 shelter, 2 adopt, 2 apartment, 2 beautiful, 2 sunset, 2 observe, 2 run, 2 breeze, 2 wheel, 2 enjoy, 2 sleep, 2 fight, 2 participles, 2 vacation, 2 down, 2 review, 2 doctor, 2 clauses, 2 few, 2 line, 2 simple, 2 continuous, 2 arriving, 2 visiting, 2 staring, 2 asking, 2 morning, 2 night, 2 suspicious, 2 ing, 2 eating, 2 million, 2 cnding, 2 agree, 2 hi, 2 places, 2 instead, 2 plane, 2 believe, 2 given, 2 late, 2 nothing, 2 wait, 2 you're, 2 wasn't, 2 special, 2 roller, 2 words, 2 man, 2 coaster, 2 gone, 2 applied, 2 earned, 2 fallen, 2 form, 2 colleges, 2 moment, 2 college, 2 saw, 2 five, 2 big, 2 degree, 2 planned, 2 coming, 2 attention, 2 graduates, 2 pendulum, 2 aren't, 2 ridden, 2 getting, 2 correct, 2 baby, 2 control, 2 pluperfect, 2 cooked, 2 didn't, 2 slides, 2 regret, 2 should, 2 laundry, 2 city, 2 second, 2 schoology, 2 favorite, 2 show, 2 ready, 2 ten, 2 worked, 2 ball, 2 describing, 2 soon, 2 finished, 2 exercise, 2 rent, 2 anything, 2 thing, 2 grandmother, 2 waited, 2 way, 2 couldn't, 2 able, 2 shouldn't, 2 did, 2 lasted, 2 almost, 2 someone, 2 face, 2 sentence, 2 travel, 2 again, 2 sharks, 2 de, 2 remember, 2 already, 2 unpublished, 2 yesterday, 2 twice, 2 satisfied, 2 lucky, 2 ex, 2 classmates, 2 voluntary, 2 even, 2 actions, 2 javier, 2 completed, 2 questionnaire, 2 promises, 2 association, 2 product, 2 students, 2 recorded, 2 videos, 2 sheets, 2 harry, 2 six, 2 shrimp, 2 crew, 2 paved, 2 stretch, 2 highway, 2 saturday, 2 tom, 2 painted, 2 choir, 2 piece, 2 forest, 2 fire, 2 destroyed, 2 suburb, 2 rose, 2 listening, 2 expressions, 2 such, 2 paragraph, 2 corrections, 2 latin, 2 saying, 2 mine, 2 celebrated, 2 united, 2 states, 2 canada, 2 ever, 2 november, 2 fall, 2 settlers, 2 sent, 2 hunt, 2 its, 2 might, 2 war, 2 once, 2 deer, 2 feast, 2 traditional, 2 modern, 2 declared, 2 dancing, 2 scientists, 2 learning, 2 speaking, 2 candy, 2 childhood, 2 age, 2 bilingualism, 2 languages, 2 dementia, 2 related, 2 both, 2 singing, 2 it'll, 2 predictions, 2 four, 2 mexico, 2 popcorn, 2 common, 2 from , 2 lyricstranslate, 2 com, 2 en, 2 html, 2 shopping, 2 road, 2 buts, 2 those, 2 wanna, 1 adjust, 1 sails, 1 seashore, 1 destination, 1 jimmi, 1 dean, 1 watch, 1 send, 1 irregular, 1 cake, 1 studied, 1 liked, 1 dessert, 1 silently, 1 takes, 1 march, 1 anniversary, 1 future , 1 ship, 1 devil's, 1 american, 1 culture, 1 means, 1 organizing, 1 agreed, 1 regular, 1 interrupted, 1 sophomore, 1 graduating, 1 bowl, 1 carefully, 1 leaving, 1 diploma, 1 smile, 1 let's, 1 enrolled, 1 play, 1 speech, 1 talking, 1 focused, 1 university, 1 smell, 1 internship, 1 soft, 1 well, 1 known, 1 firm, 1 beef, 1 immigration, 1 ocean, 1 graduation, 1 ceremony, 1 touching, 1 chicken, 1 illness, 1 sí, 1 skins, 1 definitely, 1 internships, 1 multiple, 1 er, 1 departments, 1 saved, 1 lives, 1 helped, 1 immigrants, 1 psychologist, 1 become, 1 lawyer, 1 took, 1 vegetarian, 1 oh, 1 god, 1 must, 1 body, 1 seafood, 1 drink, 1 coconut, 1 test, 1 goal, 1 levels, 1 practicing, 1 conversations, 1 classmate, 1 amanda, 1 pregnant, 1 birth, 1 water, 1 forrest, 1 teach, 1 choice, 1 auliq, 1 ice, 1 front, 1 argue, 1 cry, 1 sad, 1 mad, 1 laugh, 1 jump, 1 started, 1 job, 1 works, 1 pages, 1 example, 1 michelle's, 1 vincent, 1 enjoying, 1 g, 1 walked, 1 minute, 1 watched, 1 scarf, 1 tv, 1 interfered, 1 expressing, 1 underestimate, 1 room, 1 youngest, 1 soccer, 1 picked, 1 leaves, 1 backyard, 1 cleaning, 1 footprints, 1 floor, 1 toddler, 1 emptied, 1 clothes, 1 drawers, 1 alejandro, 1 retired, 1 managed, 1 marketing, 1 company, 1 adele, 1 lived, 1 great, 1 person, 1 woke, 1 neighbor, 1 garage, 1 wife, 1 breakfast, 1 cousin, 1 fixed, 1 cat, 1 fought, 1 si, 1 grandma, 1 grandpa, 1 mowed, 1 yard, 1 nephew, 1 broken, 1 window, 1 tennis, 1 caterpillar, 1 images, 1 sides, 1 page, 1 according, 1 letter, 1 recent, 1 adventure, 1 disaster, 1 statements, 1 context, 1 name, 1 wasting, 1 robbing, 1 oneself, 1 estonian, 1 proverb, 1 mate, 1 experience, 1 rest, 1 airplane, 1 mistakes, 1 concert, 1 denver, 1 waiting, 1 condicional, 1 tenses, 1 remembered, 1 specific, 1 throwing, 1 town, 1 cold, 1 glad, 1 rich, 1 reminding, 1 excited, 1 career, 1 super, 1 problem, 1 behind, 1 john, 1 lose, 1 turns, 1 sussy's, 1 motorcycle, 1 weight, 1 wear, 1 jose's, 1 bikini, 1 ed, 1 disappointed, 1 previews, 1 honeymoon, 1 tough, 1 resilient, 1 facts, 1 interest, 1 upset, 1 losing, 1 bracelet, 1 wooden, 1 hobby, 1 scuba, 1 diving, 1 steve, 1 further, 1 project, 1 fiji, 1 tooth, 1 paste, 1 suze, 1 carl, 1 date, 1 movies, 1 matt, 1 borrowed, 1 necklace, 1 fighting, 1 urge, 1 cookie, 1 roommate, 1 gloves, 1 half, 1 miles, 1 siblings, 1 lent, 1 wash, 1 south, 1 break, 1 theater, 1 turned, 1 carlos, 1 decided, 1 match, 1 appropriate, 1 rewrite, 1 disposition, 1 medicines, 1 jim, 1 martha's, 1 martha, 1 attraction, 1 missed, 1 fill, 1 open, 1 i'll, 1 spring, 1 opens, 1 bill, 1 leave, 1 mario, 1 expensive, 1 knew, 1 sharp, 1 teeth, 1 running, 1 longer, 1 sometimes, 1 maria, 1 comes, 1 appointment, 1 answers, 1 he'll, 1 drops, 1 fortunate, 1 pedro, 1 calderón, 1 embarrassed, 1 la, 1 barca, 1 pale, 1 difficult, 1 enough, 1 volunteer, 1 hypothetical, 1 voices, 1 noon, 1 midnight, 1 animal, 1 release, 1 formed, 1 stories, 1 negative, 1 however, 1 couple, 1 performing, 1 lottery, 1 likes, 1 playing, 1 itself, 1 does, 1 exceptions, 1 appear, 1 presentation, 1 famous, 1 chilean, 1 writer, 1 nadia, 1 bolivar, 1 presents, 1 latest, 1 achievement, 1 talks, 1 experiences, 1 spent, 1 asian, 1 photographs, 1 collected, 1 renowned, 1 newspapers, 1 reviews, 1 surprisingly, 1 himself, 1 surely, 1 bookstores, 1 around, 1 ago, 1 filled, 1 interested, 1 buying, 1 thousands, 1 copies, 1 surprise, 1 readers, 1 recommend, 1 bookstore, 1 without, 1 doubt, 1 sold, 1 hotcakes, 1 gets, 1 copy, 1 dogs, 1 e, 1 cats, 1 ee, 1 lack, 1 unchanged, 1 approves, 1 feels, 1 approved, 1 observed, 1 agreeing, 1 double, 1 consonant, 1 cvc, 1 changed, 1 sitting, 1 swim, 1 swimming, 1 put, 1 putting, 1 unspecific, 1 ie, 1 becomes, 1 clean, 1 y, 1 lie, 1 lying, 1 sorry, 1 enjoys, 1 kathy, 1 enjoyed, 1 wanted, 1 picking, 1 welcome, 1 mike, 1 identify, 1 paragraphs, 1 these, 1 wasted, 1 attractions, 1 antoine, 1 saint, 1 exupery, 1 roles, 1 awesome, 1 comprehension, 1 reading, 1 instructions, 1

amazing, 1 exciting, 1 natural, 1 conversation, 1 speed, 1 girlfriend, 1 translate, 1 opinion, 1 explain, 1 europe, 1 grammatical, 1 constructions, 1 personal, 1 opinions, 1 answer, 1 doc, 1 set, 1 guts, 1 recipies, 1 cooking, 1 simply, 1 motion, 1 word, 1 bean, 1 america, 1 latino, 1 delayed, 1 porridge, 1 with , 1 congrí , 1 rice, 1 salads, 1 sizes, 1 shapes, 1 colors, 1 york, 1 geographic, 1 table, 1 due, 1 primarily, 1 fact, 1 abandoned, 1 hotel, 1 blessing, 1 until, 1 preceding, 1 fourth, 1 thursday, 1 afraid, 1 monday, 1 october, 1 note, 1 landed, 1 mishaps, 1 certain, 1 cab, 1 crashed, 1 heard, 1 gunshots, 1 alerted, 1 leader, 1 forget, 1 invited, 1 preparing, 1 simulator, 1 settlement, 1 feeling, 1 rumor, 1 true, 1 after, 1 interesting, 1 realized, 1 hunting, 1 mom's, 1 blanks, 1 days, 1 women, 1 children, 1 meal, 1 consisted, 1 corn, 1 shellfish, 1 roasted, 1 meat, 1 today's, 1 won, 1 played, 1 games, 1 sang, 1 scared, 1 available, 1 abraham, 1 lincoln, 1 still, 1 thanksgivings, 1 august, 1 commemorate, 1 battle, 1 gettysburg, 1 general, 1 blessings, 1 peace, 1 between, 1 generation, 1 popular, 1 reverence, 1 england, 1 reminder, 1 betrayal, 1 bloodshed, 1 gathered, 1 statue, 1 plymouth, 1 massachusetts, 1 ancestors, 1 strength, 1 shaking, 1 subjuntive, 1 susan, 1 perry, 1 myself, 1 www, 1 brainfacts, 1 org, 1 sensing, 1 behaving, 1 articles, 1 neurological, 1 nervous, 1 anyone, 1 fine, 1 tonight, 1 relax, 1 benefits, 1 extend, 1 alpine, 1 attendants, 1 speak, 1 developed, 1 distinct, 1 advantages, 1 monolingual, 1 peers, 1 research, 1 neurobiology, 1 suddenly, 1 creating, 1 fluent, 1 police, 1 particularly, 1 early, 1 enhances, 1 person's, 1 ability, 1 concentrate, 1 protect, 1 against, 1 onset, 1 attitude, 1 seemed, 1 decline, 1 although, 1 why, 1 creates, 1 reserve, 1 theorize, 1 increase, 1 blood, 1 oxygen, 1 flow, 1 nerve, 1 connections, 1 healthy, 1 factors, 1 ward, 1 celebrate, 1 which, 1 funny, 1 nephews, 1 cannot, 1 focus, 1 anonymous, 1 finishes, 1 arrested, 1 improving, 1 pronunciation, 1 karaoke, 1 spend, 1 what's, 1 eyes, 1 circles, 1 windows, 1 opened, 1 atmosphere, 1 depends, 1 us, 1 worth, 1 bad, 1 checked, 1 below, 1 went, 1 passengers, 1 salsa, 1 lost, 1 boarded, 1 temptation, 1 guess, 1 though, 1 easy, 1 impossible, 1 achieved, 1 sadness, 1 you'll, 1 soul, 1 flying, 1 shine, 1 sun, 1 everyone, 1 bomb, 1 slide, 1 painting, 1 esperanza, 1 diego, 1 torres, 1 colour, 1 care, 1 ixzz3jf0sqtqm, 1 pirate, 1 box, 1 stay, 1 i'll, 1 choose, 1 ain't, 1 cause, 1 grow, 1 beach, 1 win, 1 ferris, 1 tripping, 1 vision, 1 prediction, 1 i'mma, 1 top, 1 direction, 1 decide, 1 yours, 1 compare, 1 worry, 1 alone, 1 wind, 1 bfestoy, 1 equivocado, 1 enroll,

1488 Unique Spanish Words in order of number of occurrences i.e. "de" occurs 202 times.

202 de, 190 la, 136 el, 129 que, 116 en, 95 no, 95 para, 64 y, 60 mo, 63 los, 56 yo, 52 mi, 49 ella, 49 una, 48 se, 47 por, 46 las, 42 si, 42 del, 40 lo, 36 con, 36 había, 34 pero, 33 al, 32 cuando, 30 es, 29 un, 28 como, 26 su, 26 pasado, 26 voy, 25 tu, 24 entonces, 23 he, 23 ir, 22 hacer, 22 vamos, 22 futuro, 21 lección, 21 va, 20 ellos, 20 te, 20 ha, 19 todo, 19 nos, 18 día, 18 estado, 17 clase, 17 estaba, 16 hemos, 16 han, 15 qué, 15 habré, 14 más, 14 nosotros, 14 tarea, 14 verbo, 14 tú, 14 esta, 14 compañero, 14 fue, 13 tus, 13 escribe, 13 oraciones, 13 perfecto, 13 hecho, 13 ya, 13 muy, 13 semana, 13 algo, 13 gracias, 13 acción, 13 libro, 12 siento, 12 o, 12 vida, 12 usa, 12 así, 12 equivoco, 11 tiempo, 11 historia, 11 estoy, 11 año, 11 casa, 11 voz, 10 le, 10 vocabulario, 10 actividades, 10 claves, 10 ver, 10 llegar, 10 ser, 10 mucho, 10 frases, 10 objetivo, 10 ahora, 9 fiesta, 9 son, 9 hablar, 9 presente, 9 comido, 9 visto, 9 participio, 9 puedo, 9 próximo, 9 habrá, 9 pasiva, 9 activa, 8 tener, 8 haciendo, 8 usando, 8 haber, 8 ejemplos, 8 muchas, 8 veces, 8 mañana, 8 mejor, 8 este, 8 sus, 8 puede, 7 todos, 7 planes, 7 final, 7 aprender, 7 usos, 7 sujeto, 7 cena, 7 verbos, 7 escrito, 7 hoy, 7 nunca, 7 vez, 7 cómo, 7 siempre, 7 saber, 7 fin, 7 color, 7 esperanza, 6 etc, 6 español, 6 sí, 6 viaje, 6 estás, 6 nuevas, 6 mamá, 6 practicar, 6 has, 6 antes, 6 hasta, 6 dos, 6 muchos, 6 también, 6 vas, 6 van, 6 solo, 6 durante, 6 iba, 6 escuela, 6 podría, 6 estaban, 6 estuvo, 6 sé, 6 años, 6 pluscuamperfecto, 6 trabajo, 6 toda, 6 josé, 6 cara, 5 situaciones, 5 nada, 5 fuera, 5 amiga, 5 puedes, 5 manejado, 5 ido, 5 dinero, 5 ud, 5 vosotros, 5 uds, 5 amigo, 5 hace, 5 lee, 5 desde, 5 comprar, 5 cosas, 5 anita, 5 espero, 5 está, 5 cambiar, 5 aeropuerto, 5 cada, 5 todas, 5 continuo, 5 estábamos, 5 momento, 5 gradúe, 5 menos, 5 necesito, 5 leyes, 5 sussy, 5 presidente, 5 mundo, 5 nacional, 5 pintarse, 5 tentar, 5 corazón, 4 tres, 4 aquí, 4 después, 4 otra, 4 visitado, 4 forma, 4 sin, 4 estar, 4 decir, 4 sólo, 4 mientras, 4 porque, 4 nosotras, 4 tampoco, 4 haz, 4 lista, 4 vivido, 4 mí, 4 tomar, 4 visitar, 4 primero, 4 algunos, 4 huevos, 4 uno, 4 dijo, 4 perder, 4 afuera, 4 mismo, 4 vuelo, 4 pasó, 4 creer, 4 nuestro, 4 serio, 4 preguntas, 4 cuéntale, 4 tuviera, 4 aprendido, 4 sobre, 4 empezar, 4 preparado, 4 hija, 4 esposo, 4 nuevo, 4 situación, 4 evento, 4 sido, 4 acerca, 4 inglés, 4 poder, 4 amigos, 4 japón, 4 será, 4 frijoles, 4 cosecha, 4 celebración, 4 massasoit, 4 nativos, 4 querer, 4 pueda, 4 dar, 4 intentar, 4 razón, 3 comer, 3 quien, 3 mes, 3 usar, 3 posible, 3 abuela, 3 unos, 3 atención, 3 personas, 3 parque, 3 diversiones, 3 pagar, 3 tazas, 3 té, 3 maíz, 3 niños, 3 creo, 3 tenemos, 3 infinitivo, 3 bailar, 3 junio, 3 ayudar, 3 cuáles, 3 disfrutar, 3 verano, 3 tengo, 3 tamales, 3 frescos, 3 país, 3 algunas, 3 gente, 3 apartamento, 3 comida, 3 bien, 3 vacaciones, 3 completa, 3 propios, 3 próxima, 3 llegado, 3 todavía, 3 preferiría, 3 clima, 3 progresivo, 3 siguientes, 3 abordando, 3 expresar, 3 pude, 3 grave, 3 tanto, 3 iría, 3 dices, 3 mis, 3 hora, 3 importante, 3 preparatoria, 3 segundo, 3 estudiante, 3 prepa, 3 diploma, 3 universidad, 3 realmente, 3 quiere, 3 medicina, 3 estudiantes, 3 bebé, 3 galletas, 3 ropa, 3 perro, 3 hijo, 3 otro, 3 varios, 3 llama, 3 verbales, 3 vencido, 3 ponerse, 3 plantado, 3 circo, 3 tuvo, 3 era, 3 camino, 3 crea, 3 recomendado, 3 eclipse, 3 autografiadas, 3 enfatizar, 3 autora, 3 fueron, 3 tan, 3 idioma, 3 pudiera, 3 wampanoag, 3 hombres, 3 americanos, 3 cerebro, 3 bilingüe, 3 http, 3 edad, 3 quitarse, 3 miedos, 3 sacarlos, 3 podríamos, 3 intentando, 3 dejes, 2 esto, 2 schoology, 2 describiendo, 2 lugar, 2 simple, 2 casar, 2 conjugaciones, 2 cine, 2 noche, 2 cuatro, 2 largo, 2 alguien, 2 carrera, 2 están, 2 gustaría, 2 encantan, 2 carne, 2 ayer, 2 tejer, 2 sabe, 2 invierno, 2 allá, 2 voluntarias, 2 refugio, 2 animales, 2 gustan, 2 ar, 2 hombre, 2 pintar, 2 expresiones, 2 playa, 2 sentar, 2 atardecer, 2 reír, 2 correr, 2 briza, 2 sentir, 2 nuestra, 2 dormir, 2 demasiado, 2 e, 2 feliz, 2 er, 2 parte, 2 crear, 2 siguiente, 2 significa, 2 llegando, 2 visitando, 2 diferentes, 2 mirando, 2 pasada, 2 estabas, 2 ese, 2 sospechosa, 2 caminando, 2 tiempos, 2 hola, 2 cuéntame, 2 lugares, 2 ti, 2 acá, 2 loco, 2 montaña, 2 debido, 2 rusa, 2 caído, 2 carro, 2 especial, 2 imagino, 2 tarde, 2 haya, 2 pronto, 2 embargo, 2 demás, 2 incómoda, 2 corta, 2 palabras, 2 lograr, 2 péndulo, 2 aplicado, 2 montado, 2 tienen, 2 entrado, 2 recibido, 2 habremos, 2 habrás, 2 lotería, 2 planear, 2 comparte, 2 estudiando, 2 participios, 2 universidades, 2 propias, 2 termine, 2 grande, 2 compañía, 2 reciba, 2 deslizaderos, 2 graduemos, 2 cambie, 2 ciudad, 2 compañeros, 2 quisiera, 2 mareado, 2 lavado, 2 mareada, 2 millón, 2 habíamos, 2 habían, 2 llegué, 2 dulces, 2 limpiado, 2 práctica, 2 limpiar, 2 dejado, 2 palomitas, 2 casado, 2 gran, 2 persona, 2 sobrino, 2 entre, 2 pelota, 2 peros, 2 nueva, 2 otros, 2 méxico, 2 anhelando, 2 dio, 2 abandonar, 2 recogiera, 2 dejó, 2 alegro, 2 sacar, 2 supo, 2 pidió, 2 varias, 2 bailado, 2 esperó, 2 echó, 2 ponerme, 2 cita, 2 devolvió, 2 casi, 2 días, 2 cualquier, 2 frase, 2 nuevamente, 2 tiene, 2 estaré, 2 dejará, 2 sabía, 2 tiburones, 2 esperar, 2 anticipación, 2 dejar, 2 inéditas, 2 rueda, 2 lanzamiento, 2 satisfecha, 2 afortunados, 2 ej, 2 cuenta, 2 fila, 2 copias, 2 javier, 2 cuestionario, 2 asociación, 2 alimentos, 2 producto, 2 videos, 2 sábanas, 2 semanas, 2 harry, 2 seis, 2 camarones, 2 tripulación, 2 tramo, 2 carretera, 2 sábado, 2 tom, 2 coro, 2 esa, 2 pieza, 2 incendio, 2 forestal, 2 barrio, 2 cambia, 2 leer, 2 párrafo, 2 pregúntale, 2 pensar, 2 celebra, 2 canadá, 2 avión, 2 noviembre, 2 colonos, 2 buscar, 2 ingleses, 2 guerra, 2 juntos, 2 sangre, 2 científicos, 2 cognitivos, 2 bilingüismo, 2 idiomas, 2 demencia, 2 aunque, 2 comunes, 2 hay, 2 andar, 2 vale, 2 mas, 2 haría, 2 lyricstranslate, 2 com, 2 html, 2 equivocado, 2 llamó, 2 vemos, 2 quiero, 2 agregando, 1 aterrizamos, 1 tuve, 1 calamidades, 1 madre, 1 cuéntamelo, 1 rico, 1 taxi, 1 chocó, 1 denver, 1 frío, 1 les, 1 cometiendo, 1 impediría, 1 llegaste, 1 llevarle, 1 eso, 1 asustados, 1 wooden, 1 seguía, 1 temblando, 1 nervioso, 1 nadie, 1 guantes, 1 relájate, 1 espera, 1 contado, 1 azafatas, 1 fijamente, 1 hermanos, 1 policía, 1 actitud, 1 pareció, 1 sur, 1 inventando, 1 digas, 1 llevaron, 1 detenido, 1 distinto, 1 revisaron, 1 frente, 1 adónde, 1 pasajeros, 1 veían, 1 trajeras, 1 bomba, 1 llevaré, 1 ciertos, 1 alguna, 1 compraría, 1 incomoda, 1 hayas, 1 invéntate, 1 harías, 1 medicinas, 1

dirección, 1 viento, 1 ajustar, 1 velas, 1 costosas, 1 destino, 1 jimmi, 1 dean, 1 difíciles, 1 encontrar, 1 habré , 1 concierto, 1 ejercicios, 1 cenar, 1 arrepiéntete, 1 vais, 1 perros, 1 habréis, 1 habrán, 1 pastel, 1 estudiado, 1 pasar, 1 gatos, 1 condicional, 1 marzo, 1 aniversario, 1 comprarías, 1 presta, 1 siente, 1 comerías, 1 cultura, 1 americana, 1 organizar, 1 lástima, 1 manera, 1 veo, 1 aquellos, 1 pudiste, 1 espacios, 1 planeando, 1 graduarme, 1 imprevisto, 1 dije, 1 abandonado, 1 acordé, 1 venir, 1 den, 1 esas, 1 temo, 1 recordé, 1 matriculado, 1 abajo, 1 mantengo, 1 pudieras, 1 concentrado, 1 estudiar, 1 graduado, 1 adoptar, 1 prácticas, 1 vincent, 1 conocida, 1 g, 1 abogados, 1 ejercicio, 1 teléfono, 1 pedirá, 1 inmigración, 1 planeado, 1 ceremonia, 1 graduación, 1 irregulares, 1 unir, 1 ayuda, 1 cuentas, 1 residencia, 1 múltiples, 1 departamentos, 1 emergencias, 1 salvado, 1 vidas, 1 ayudado, 1 justo, 1 unirse, 1 psicóloga, 1 convirtamos, 1 médico, 1 abogado, 1 mandaría, 1 dios, 1 santo, 1 empiezo, 1 próximos, 1 gastarme, 1 correcta, 1 examen, 1 duro, 1 meta, 1 terminar, 1 niveles, 1 practicando, 1 conversaciones, 1 telefónicas, 1 llamar, 1 amanda, 1 embarazada, 1 luz, 1 hermosa, 1 par, 1 forrest, 1 toma, 1 control, 1 tomando, 1 decisión, 1 sobrinos, 1 auliq, 1 ice, 1 hablando, 1 terminemos, 1 fueran, 1 emocionante, 1 york, 1 contigo, 1 bonito, 1 encantar, 1 empezado, 1 errores, 1 decidí, 1 eventos, 1 ocurre, 1 revisa, 1 páginas, 1 repasar, 1 formas, 1 volver, 1 habías, 1 habíais, 1 orilla, 1 ejemplo, 1 cortas, 1 salió, 1 veremos, 1 salido, 1 ocurrió, 1 pretérito, 1 llegó, 1 caminado, 1 queremos, 1 ve, 1 programa, 1 favorito, 1 silenciosamente, 1 habitación, 1 menor, 1 observar, 1 futbol, 1 recogido, 1 hojas, 1 patio, 1 trasero, 1 terminé, 1 cuidadosamente, 1 hijos, 1 huellas, 1 piso, 1 sacado, 1 reciente, 1 cajones, 1 pedido, 1 ganarte, 1 alejandro, 1 pensionó, 1 mercadeo, 1 jugar, 1 ganado, 1 vine, 1 trabajado, 1 dicho, 1 oler, 1 subjuntivo, 1 desperté, 1 vecino, 1 garaje, 1 esposa, 1 desayuno, 1 suave, 1 reparado, 1 gato, 1 peleado, 1 océano, 1 abuelo, 1 cortado, 1 césped, 1 roto, 1 ventana, 1 ustedes, 1 tenis, 1 imágenes, 1 ambos, 1 lados, 1 página, 1 carta, 1 tocar, 1 desastre, 1 ellas, 1 nombre, 1 desperdiciar, 1 robarse, 1 proverbio, 1 estonia, 1 tuvieras, 1 impidió, 1 experiencia, 1 resto, 1 piel, 1 definitivamente, 1 supo , 1 mucha, 1 específicas, 1 poner, 1 mar, 1 mareados, 1 llegará, 1 diferente, 1 agua, 1 coco, 1 aventura, 1 unas, 1 vuelto, 1 renta, 1 pelear, 1 viviste, 1 discutir, 1 acompañara, 1 mal, 1 cansando, 1 recordarle, 1 punto, 1 idea, 1 emocionado, 1 pensado, 1 problema, 1 atrasado, 1 llorar, 1 apenada, 1 trabajó, 1 ratito, 1 abandonó, 1 listo, 1 llegara, 1 triste, 1 vino, 1 resulta, 1 motocicleta, 1 pálida, 1 vieja, 1 molestar, 1 bailando, 1 pudo, 1 podía, 1 comunicarse, 1 desilusionados, 1 podemos, 1 tobogán, 1 anteriores, 1 deberías, 1 renunciar, 1 duros, 1 acaban, 1 resistente, 1 sigue, 1 divertido, 1 nuevos, 1 hechos, 1 interesan, 1 molestó, 1 perdió, 1 pulsera, 1 superé, 1 mantén, 1 buen, 1 pensando, 1 hobby, 1 piensas, 1 bucear, 1 steve, 1 encuentra, 1 avanzado, 1 proyecto, 1 olvidar, 1 usaste, 1 acabaste, 1 pasta, 1 dental, 1 suze, 1 carl, 1 primera, 1 loca, 1 deberían, 1 películas, 1 hayan, 1 quieres, 1 revelar, 1 matt, 1 prestado, 1 collar, 1 saltar, 1 luchando, 1 contra, 1 ganas, 1 comerme, 1 galleta, 1 di, 1 coche, 1 alcanzó, 1 haga, 1 medio, 1 millas, 1 cosa, 1 dejarás, 1 cuaresma, 1 lavo, 1 querías, 1 llamarlo, 1 saldrán, 1 imperfecciones, 1 esperando, 1 expectativa, 1 buena, 1 sacaste, 1 dejarte, 1 resultó, 1 difícil, 1 dejarla, 1 carlos, 1 parada, 1 ojo, 1 minuto, 1 verbal, 1 adecuada, 1 espacio, 1 luego, 1 redacta, 1 próximas, 1 antiguamente, 1 debo, 1 jim, 1 tenía, 1 pertenecía, 1 marta, 1 cuerpo, 1 eché, 1 abierto, 1 promesas, 1 abra, 1 primavera, 1 bill, 1 llevará, 1 acciones, 1 allí, 1 mario, 1 use, 1 cerca, 1 expresando, 1 leyó, 1 dientes, 1 afilados, 1 corrí, 1 agoté, 1 continuar, 1 maría, 1 viene, 1 visitarme, 1 programada, 1 respuestas, 1 devolver, 1 predicciones, 1 subestimes, 1 adele, 1 trata, 1 echarse, 1 llega, 1 oficina, 1 afortunado, 1 pedro, 1 calderón, 1 barca, 1 compuestos, 1 piensa, 1 divertida, 1 ayudarte, 1 acordar, 1 compuesto, 1 significado, 1 compártelo, 1 querría, 1 salsa, 1 iríamos, 1 elaborar, 1 llevar, 1 alpino, 1 invitara, 1 suficientes, 1 doctor, 1 viajar, 1 ferris, 1 oruga, 1 quién, 1 realizando, 1 letras, 1 interesantes, 1 terminado, 1 recomendó, 1 menudo, 1 ni, 1 siquiera, 1 aparece, 1 famosa, 1 escritora, 1 chilena, 1 nadia, 1 bolívar, 1 presenta, 1 obra, 1 graduar, 1 numerosas, 1 vivencias, 1 impiden, 1 asiático, 1 fotografías, 1 recopiladas, 1 sentirse, 1 destacados, 1 diarios, 1 buenas, 1 críticas, 1 sorprendentemente, 1 mismísimo, 1 seguramente, 1 librerías, 1 respectivas, 1 estarán, 1 repletas, 1 interesada, 1 miles, 1 peso, 1 sorpresa, 1 lectores, 1 recomendamos, 1 visite, 1 librería, 1 favorita, 1 dudar, 1 arriendo, 1 vendido, 1 pan, 1 caliente, 1 usted, 1 bikini, 1 completó, 1 case, 1 completado, 1 luna, 1 locas, 1 miel, 1 aprueba, 1 fiji, 1 aprobado, 1 observará, 1 observado, 1 grabaron, 1 compras, 1 atracción, 1 grabados, 1 cambio, 1 irías, 1 veamos, 1 cambiadas, 1 soy, 1 comió, 1 pensé, 1 imperfecto, 1 comidos, 1 funciona, 1 pavimento, 1 escribir, 1 falta, 1 pavimentado, 1 pasaron, 1 limpiada, 1 cláusulas, 1 pintó, 1 pintada, 1 hablaría, 1 disfruto, 1 importa, 1 anoche, 1 disfrutada, 1 especificar, 1 discurso, 1 destruyó, 1 afirmación, 1 destruido, 1 identifica, 1 párrafos, 1 oración, 1 utiliza, 1 estos, 1 pasaste, 1 rosa, 1 hizo, 1 otras, 1 antoine, 1 saint, 1 exupery, 1 trabaja, 1 pídele, 1 mediodía, 1 roles, 1 auditiva, 1 escuchar, 1 comprender, 1 medianoche, 1 instrucciones, 1 atracciones, 1 nativo, 1 velocidad, 1 natural, 1 conversación, 1 gastó, 1 pide, 1 traduzca, 1 acabas, 1 ando, 1 opinión, 1 corrige, 1 explícale, 1 corrección, 1 correcciones, 1 construcción, 1 gramatical, 1 opiniones, 1 responde, 1 documento, 1 simulador, 1 latinos, 1 recetas, 1 cocina, 1 iendo, 1 latinoamerica, 1 latino, 1 frecuencia, 1 comen, 1 mía, 1 degustamos, 1 diario, 1 maneras, 1 potajes, 1 arroz, 1 congrí, 1 ensaladas, 1 verdad, 1 tantas, 1 variedades, 1 pues, 1 cansamos, 1 comerlos, 1 acaso, 1 pasa, 1 dia, 1 accion, 1 national, 1 geographic, 1 ado, 1 principalmente, 1 estados, 1 unidos, 1 comiendo, 1 bendición, 1 jugando, 1 anterior, 1 cuarto, 1 jueves, 1 excepción, 1 ee, 1 uu, 1 lunes, 1 octubre, 1 distintos, 1 otoño, 1 yendo, 1 enviados, 1 estabais, 1 movimiento, 1 escuchó, 1 disparos, 1 alertó, 1 líder, 1 clausulas, 1 pensaban, 1 enfermedad, 1 podrían, 1 estarse, 1 preparando, 1 preparar, 1 visitó, 1 asentamiento, 1 interrumpidos, 1 rumor, 1 cierto, 1 poco, 1 visita, 1 expresan, 1 cláusula, 1 dieron, 1 cazando, 1 envió, 1 cazar, 1 ciervos, 1 mujeres, 1 comieron, 1 arrepientas, 1 consistió, 1 venado, 1 mariscos, 1 asada, 1 lejos, 1 tradicional, 1 jugaron, 1 juegos, 1 cantaron, 1 bailaron, 1 mayoría, 1 estadounidenses, 1 consumen, 1 moderno, 1 disponible, 1 abraham, 1 lincoln, 1 declaró, 1 thanksgivings, 1 nacionales, 1 agosto, 1 conmemorar, 1 batalla, 1 gettysburg, 1 bendiciones, 1 generales, 1 paz, 1 duró, 1 generación, 1 pueblo, 1 reverencia, 1 popular, 1 tradición, 1 inglaterra, 1 recuerdo, 1 traición, 1 derramamiento, 1 kathy, 1 indígenas, 1 reunido, 1 estatua, 1 plymouth, 1 massachusetts, 1 recordar, 1 antepasados, 1 fortaleza, 1 barco, 1 pirata, 1 susan, 1 perry, 1 diablo, 1 www, 1 brainfacts, 1 org, 1 sensing, 1 thinking, 1 behaving, 1 language, 1 articles, 1 bilingual, 1 brain, 1 ganara, 1 neurológicos, 1 encontrando, 1 beneficios, 1 recogerme, 1 extienden, 1 niñez, 1 juntas, 1 adulta, 1 hablas, 1 algún, 1 quizás, 1 desarrollado, 1 ventajas, 1 distinguen, 1 monolingües, 1 investigaciones, 1 neurobiología, 1 mike, 1 encontrado, 1 fluido, 1 michelle, 1 particularmente, 1 temprana, 1 mejora, 1 habilidad, 1 concentrarse, 1 sino, 1 proteja, 1 inicio, 1 maravilloso, 1 declives, 1 relacionados, 1 preste, 1 saben, 1 reserva, 1 cognitiva, 1 teorizan, 1 incrementar, 1 flujo, 1 oxígeno, 1 mantener, 1 conexiones, 1 nerviosas, 1 saludables, 1 factores, 1 piensan, 1 ayudan, 1 evitar, 1 prefieres, 1 celebras, 1 declaro, 1 opinas, 1 relacionada, 1 deja, 1 pon, 1 anonimo, 1 léele, 1 acuerden, 1 llamada, 1 hablen, 1 cantando, 1 mejorar, 1 pronunciación, 1 karaoke, 1 pollo, 1 llena, 1 increíbles, 1 ojos, 1 mirar, 1 estas, 1 cansado, 1 estuve, 1 caminar, 1 girando, 1 ventanas, 1 pueden, 1 abrir, 1 aire, 1 depende, 1 ayudará, 1 novia, 1 pena, 1 europa, 1 habéis, 1 hipotéticas, 1 cansada, 1 vegetarianos, 1 puesto, 1 inventaron, 1 historias, 1 usualmente, 1 perderse, 1 embarcar, 1 tentarse, 1 john, 1 ves, 1 fácil, 1 imposible, 1 tristeza, 1 algun, 1 irá, 1 asi, 1 cambiará, 1 sentirás, 1 alma, 1 vuela, 1 cantar, 1 brillar, 1 sol, 1 tomado, 1 enseñar, 1 divertir, 1 diego, 1 torres, 1 colour, 1 hope, 1 disposición, 1 ixzz3jf0w4u00, 1 preguntó, 1 agallas, 1 caja, 1 donde, 1 quedo, 1 elegiré, 1 intento, 1 hacen, 1 dónde, 1 crecería, 1 mío, 1 llamo, 1 hogar, 1 retrasó, 1 regresaremos, 1 tropezado, 1 visión, 1 predicción, 1 cima, 1 mires, 1 hacía, 1 atrás, 1 decidas, 1 bufanda, 1 controlen, 1 lucha, 1 tuyos, 1 compraren, 1 preocupes, 1 sola, 1 sentimos, 1 salí, 1 hotel, 1 taken, 1 from , 1 am, 1 i, 1 wrong, 1 pares, 1 regístrate, ,